Words The Sea Gave Us

Grace Tierney

Also by Grace Tierney

Nonfiction

"How To Get Your Name In The Dictionary"

Fiction

"Hamster Stew & Other Stories"
"Nit Roast & Other Stories"
"The Librarian's Secret Diary"

First published by Wordfoolery Press, 2020

Cover Design by Peter Sheehan Studio

ISBN-13: 978-1999977627

Contents

1. Parts of a Ship   6

2. Old Sea Dog Yarns   44

3. Underwater   54

4. Crew   65

5. Sounds Fishy to Me   79

6. Surfer Slang   86

7. Sea Monsters   89

8. Maritime Manoeuvres   98

9. Eponymous Words from the Sea   105

10. I Do Like to Be Beside the Seaside   122

11. Sails   134

12. Scurvy Pirates   148

13. Maps & Navigation   161

14. Sea Battles   176

15. Running a Tight Ship   183

16. Flying the Flag   190

17. Maritime Fashion   202

18. Nautical Phrases   206

19. Weather   238

20. Salmagundi   246

Index   265

Introduction

I must begin this book with a confession. I can't sail, I can't swim, and I get sick-sea thinking about floating.

However, having grown up within earshot of the curlews, with sand between my toes, and a sea mist in my hair, I am a complete coastal addict. Any day with a glimpse, or sniff, of the ocean is a good day. I lurk around lighthouses, follow lifeboats on twitter, and hold a romantic notion of cutlass-wielding pirates close to my heart.

Researching this book wasn't difficult as my house already *creaks at the seams* (see Nautical Phrases chapter) with books about everything from mermaids to commercial fishing fleets and in some ways I've been fishing words from the sea all my life.

As I delved deeper I realised we all have heads filled with phrases and words the sea gave us. Who hasn't resolved to *clear the decks* in our office or asked a noisy child to *pipe down*? The sea covers more of our planet than the land and it unites our countries and peoples. Ireland, my homeland, has territorial waters which are ten times larger than her landmass and a rich tradition of seafaring.

The further I explored the waves (with my feet firmly on dry land) the more I realised that without sailors English would be a very poor language indeed.

Fishermen, explorers, sailors, and merchants brought wealth, spices, tasty food, and words as their cargo. They discovered new words wherever they dropped anchor and English is all the richer for it.

There is one danger lurking in these wordy waters – not a giant squid or a dangerous current, but the sailor's urge to give a nautical origin to any word or phrase that sounds even vaguely seagoing. I've done my best to avoid such bait, cutting out *stow, reel, mess, armed to the teeth, drift, three square meals, abyss,* and even *rock the boat* in the process. If your favourite shipboard expression isn't here it's either been used ashore first, or it slipped through my net.

Now put on your floatation device, grab a cutlass, and join me on a voyage of exploration among the words the sea gave us.

1. Parts of a Ship

If you're a sailor you may wish to skip this section. You'll already know what a *baggywinkle* protects, that *giving a wide berth* relates to bears (yes, really), and the differences between *tun, tonne,* and *tonnage.*

If, like me, you usually skim the nautical terms in novels and wouldn't know your *halyards* from your *binnacle* then it's time to wander around a ship and find out what they call the pointy bit at the front.

Not all these terms originated at sea. They're included so you know how to talk your way around a sailing ship.

As sail names are a rich source for the English language they have their own chapter.

Aft

The back, or stern, of the vessel. This word comes from *aeftan* in Old English which means from behind "or "furthest back". It's related to *afterword* but not to *after.*

Anchor

Anchor's nautical use pre-dates the idea of *anchoring* something ashore (1300s), or a *news anchor* (1965), *anchorman* in relay racing (1934), and *anchor* in a tug-of-war team (1903) by centuries. *Ancor* entered Old English in the 800s from Latin *ancora* and Greek *anykra.*

The original Greek word is related to *anklos* (bend) which is also a source for *ankle* and *angle*.

There are many forms of *anchor*, depending on conditions. The *sheet anchor* is the largest but there's also *bower anchors* and *kedge anchors*.

Baggywinkle

A *baggywinkle*, whose word origins are uncertain, is a soft cover placed over a rope on a sailing vessel to prevent sail damage. A *baggywinkle* is a clever sailor's improvisation as it is created from old frayed ropes to protect new ropes from fraying.

Now if you're strolling around a harbour or marina and spot a shaggy rope cushion strapped to some rigging you can point knowledgeably and say "See that? That's a *baggywinkle*" and wait for your companion to either look impressed or burst out laughing.

Ballast

When a landlubber is heading out for a few drinks they may be advised to pace themselves in order to avoid a hangover. Drink plenty of water, don't mix grape and grain, carry some *ballast*.

Ballast is the heavy items stowed in the hold to stop the ship from rolling too much in a heavy sea. *Ballast* has taken many forms over the years. Concrete ballast is used now but the older version – large stones – are sometimes found abandoned on shorelines or incorporated in paving and walls at the coast.

Sometimes aircraft, hot air balloons, and even racing cars will use *ballast* to keep themselves in trim. Larger ships may have *ballast tanks* which are filled with seawater but these have contributed to ecological issues when the water is flushed out later, bringing non-native micro-species to new environments.

Ballast entered English from Middle English around 1520. Middle English had the word *bar* (to carry) and *last* (a load or burden). Interestingly there were near identical terms around the same period in North Sea German and Old Danish *barlast*. Sadly the idea that *ballast* comes from the Dutch *balg-last*, literally a belly load, isn't likely, although it would tie in with the idea of *ballast* for hangover-prevention.

In the 1800s, cargo boats returning from Europe to North America carried quarried stone as *ballast* which contributed to the built heritage of east coast cities such as Montreal.

White stones have a special significance in *ballast* in Britain and Ireland. Since the Stone Age white stones have been associated with grave sites there with some found in tombs. At more recent Christian era burials the stones may be arranged in a the shape of a cross or built into a stone cairn over a grave.

As a result, white stones were typically removed from *ballast* before loading on ships. On Clare Island, off Galway, in the 1930s the local ferryman and fishermen steadfastly refused to carry a load of white stones over to the island for the new priest to decorate the graveyard because it would jinx the boats.

Belay

If you watch enough seafaring movies, or indeed "Star Trek" episodes, you'll eventually hear a captain say

"*Belay* that order" to their crew. The order will be paused, but why?

The answer lies in the Age of Sail and with one small piece of wooden equipment. The captain is referring to the *belaying* pin, a wooden peg, something akin to a rolling pin, around which a line could be made fast (and stopped). A series of such pins were typically positioned along the ship's rail. Basically the captain is saying – "tie up that order for the moment".

Belay (1540s) comes from the Old English word *belecgan* which meant to lay a thing about, thus describing how you would lay the rope around the *belaying* pin.

Belaying is also used in mountain climbing terminology from the same source.

It is tempting to associate the over-used office phrase *put a pin in it* with the *belaying* pin as both refer to postponing a task however the pin in that phrase is widely accepted to have been the pin of a hand grenade in World War Two where putting the pin back in deferred the explosion.

A *belaying pin* was a common improvised weapon aboard a ship as they were close to hand and about the right size and weight to be used as a club.

Berth

Berth can describe a place for a sailor or passenger to sleep, but can also describe where the ship itself can be at home - a *berth* at a pier, harbour, or anchorage, for example. *Berthing* can also be a verb – the act of bringing the ship into its *berth*.

Berthing a ship was the original meaning, the idea of a sailor or passenger having a *berth* came along later, from the 1700s.

In the same way that English merges heal, or hale, with -th to give us health, and strong with -th to give us strength, it appears that *bear* was merged with *-th* to give us *berth*. Of course *bear* can be an animal or the verb to carry.

In this case it appears likely that it is the animal who gave us the word. Although *bears* can swim and enjoy the water, they're hardly aquatic creatures, but the idea is closest to the phrase *give something a wide berth*. The ship coming into dock at its *berth* needed to have enough room to do so. One of the earliest definitions, Bailey's Dictionary in the 1620s, says *berth* means "convenient sea room" for ships.

If you've ever seen a small rowing boat near a large ferry trying to dock at a pier you would understand why giving the ferry a wide *berth* would be a smart move on behalf of the row boat's crew. It's much the same distance a smart hiker would give a *bear* if they met one in the woods.

Below & Beneath

A sailor will never say they are going down to a lower deck in a ship. They will always refer to *going below*. Legend has it that saying down was bad luck on a ship as it reminded sailors of going down to the bottom of the sea or a ship going down (i.e. sinking).

Below has changed since joining English in the 1300s. The older version is *alow* (like aloft, ashore, aground etc) and *below* was a rarely used word in Middle English and only gained ground in the 1500s. You'd be more likely to hear *beneath* used instead. *Beneath* was used as a term for off-duty sailors. If they were working they were on deck (even if they were working in the hold) and if they weren't they were *beneath* (even if they were whittling a toy while perched high in the rigging).

Bilge

The *bilge* on a ship is the lowest point of a ship's inner hull. It is also the term for the dank water which collects there and is expelled by use of a *bilge pump*. *Bilge* is also used as a term to describe anything foul or nonsensical.

Bilge entered English in the 1510s as a variant of *bulge* which described a ship's curving hull or a leather bag, presumably *bulging* with its contents. *Bilge* comes from Old North French word *boulge*, Gaulish *bulga*, and Late Latin *bulga* all of which mean a leather sack.

Binnacle

A *binnacle* is the wooden housing for a ship's compass. Captain Jack Sparrow carries his magical compass about with him in a wooden box but typically a ship's compass is on the bridge neatly nested in a *binnacle* ready for use. The last thing you want is the compass to go missing, or worse, overboard in a storm.

Why wooden? Compasses use magnetism so metal probably wouldn't be a great idea, unless they are non-magnetic metal. Brass isn't magnetic which is why it's often used for metal fittings shipboard.

The word history of *binnacle* is a mini history of seafaring. The Romans gave us *habitaculum* as the word for dwelling place from the Latin verb *habitare* (to inhabit). It's easy to see its influence on modern words such as *habitation* or *inhabit*.

The next step is *bitácula* (Spanish) and *bitacola* (Portugese) and *bittacle* (Old English) by the 1620s. Those are all cousin words and yes they all mean *binnacle* because by this point – high in the Age of Sail – these three nations, and their huge merchant and naval fleets, were exploring the world on ships and needed compasses to do so.

By the 1700s, all three words had merged, in English at least, to become *binnacle* – the little wooden dwelling place for the compass on a ship.

Boom

The *boom* on a ship is a long pole or spar and entered English in the 1640s. *Boom* came to English from Scottish *boun*, which in turn was a borrowing from the Dutch word *boom* for a tree or pole. It is now used in film & TV work as a term for the fuzzy sound mike called a *boom,* or the bar to which it is attached.

A ship's boom is unrelated to the earlier word *boom* (mid 1400s) for a sound or an explosion of economic activity. That one came from the sound of bees buzzing.

Bow

The *bow* is the front of the ship where the sides curve in to a point. The word dates to the 1300s and comes from the Old Norse word *bogr* and Middle Low German *boog*, and Middle Dutch *boech* all of which have connection to bending or curved objects.

It pre-dates the use of the word *bow* to indicate bending the body as an indication of respect but it probably didn't give us that usage, they just came from similar sources.

Bowsprit

The *bowsprit* of a sailing vessel is a spar which extends forward from the prow, basically it's a pointy bit at the front. It exists so you can attach more sails at the front of the ship. Some modern racing yachts have a retractable *bowsprit*.

The word *bowsprit* is believed to originate from the Middle Low German word *bochspret* which is formed from *boch* (bow of a ship) and *spret* (pole).

The *bowsprit* is attached at an upwards angle, rather than straight out, to avoid dipping crew and sails on it into salt water during heavy seas.

Bridge

The *bridge*, as used in "Star Trek", is the centre of command on a ship and it dates back to the mid 1800s when the *bridge* was a structure stretching across the vessel, very like a *footbridge*, between or just in front of paddle wheels on a steam ship where an officer could direct the motion of the ship. This raised platform became the spot where the captain issued his orders.

In this case the word *bridge* came from land to sea, rather than vice versa. The word *bridge* originates in old words for beam or log. Presumably the original *footbridge* was walking over a fallen tree to cross a river. The words then move through German, Dutch, Norse, and Saxon spellings to reach English.

Brig

Brig is naval slang for a prison on board ship. Legend has it that during the Napoleonic Wars (1803-1815) Admiral Nelson used his *brigantine* ships as floating jails for his Spanish and French prisoners. This use of *brigs* stuck and is still used in the U.S. Navy today, and on "Star Trek" which models many of its terms on sailing ship jargon.

Bulkhead

A *bulkhead* is a vertical partition in the interior of a ship and has been in English since the 1400s. It's a compound word of *bulk* and *head*. The *bulk* was a framework and may come from the Old Norse *bolkr* (beam, rafter, or partition).

A *bulkhead* is designed both to sub-divide space below decks but also to add structure and rigidity to the design. Having *bulkheads* can slow the spread of fire or water but was typically removed if the vessel was used by pirates as they wanted to maximise storage space for booty.

The doomed passenger liner the *Titanic* had sixteen flotation compartments and was designed to stay afloat even with four of them flooded. Unfortunately the *bulkheads* between the compartments were not tall enough to contain the water that rushed in when she hit the iceberg and she sank in two and a half hours.

Bumpkin

A *bumpkin* is a spar projecting out from the hull of a vessel. The *bumpkin* is like a *bowsprit* (explained above) but in this case there would be four of them, one from each quarter of the ship.

On shore the word describes a *country bumpkin*, a simple rustic country-living person. The Dutch word *boomken* refers to a short stumpy man or a little tree and may be the original source for *bumpkin* linguistically. The vertically challenged *country bumpkin* entered English as a derogatory term for a Dutch man in the 1500s, but it originated in nautical use.

Bunk

A *bunk* is a sleeping berth on board ship, sometimes with raised sides to prevent the sleeper rolling out during heavy seas. The word moved from ships to railways and later to *bunk beds* as a way of fitting extra sleeping spaces into bedrooms. The word *bunk* can now also be used as a verb, since the 1800s, meaning to occupy a bed. There's also the idea of a *bunkhouse*.

Bunk, which entered English in the 1700s, is likely to be a shortening of *bunker* which was originally a Scottish word for a seat or bench. Golf *bunkers* arrived in the 1800s and fortified *bunkers* came along in World War I.

Cabin

Cabin has two definitions in the dictionary – a private space on a ship or a structure in the wilderness - and both come with the adjective of small. *Cabins* at sea are rarely spacious but they do provide some privacy.

Both definitions of the word arose in English in the mid 1300s so it's unclear which *cabin* came first – on shore or afloat. Its origins are also somewhat unclear but are likely to be from Late Latin *capanna* (hut) and then via *cabane* in Old French to English.

The related term – *cabin-fever* – has a genuine medical history. In the 1820s it was used to describe typhus but by 1918 is had acquired its modern sense of an urge to get out and about.

Cable

A *cable* in nautical use is a rope of more than ten inches in diameter used to hold the ship at its moorings. *Cable* reached English in the 1100s as large and strong rope or chain used on a ship. *Cable* had travelled to English from Latin *capulum* (rope or halter for cattle) via Old North French *cable*.

Cable has shoreside uses too. A *cable* on land is more likely to be made of wire rather than hemp or fibres. From the 1850s a *cable* was part of telegraphy (although sending a telegram rather than a *cable* remained more used in British English) and from the 1880s in railroads. *Cable* television arrived in 1963.

Caboose

A *caboose* was a small galley cabin on deck for cooking in the 1700s. The word comes from Middle Dutch *kambuis* (ship's galley). In the 1850s the word transferred ashore as the American English term for the carriage/car on a train used by the conductor and brakeman.

Capstan

Similar to the windlass (see below), this mechanism is a revolving cylinder used for winding a rope or cable, developed to multiply the efforts of the sailors in hauling up the anchor, for example. *Capstan* sea shanties were songs sung to encourage the crew when turning the *capstan*.

A *capstan* is also the name for a rotating shaft in a tape recording device for turning the tape at a regular speed.

Capstan entered English in the 1300s from Old French *cabestant* and ultimately from Latin *capere* meaning to hold or take.

Cargo

Cargo are the goods transported by ship, airplane, or vehicle.

The roots of the word *cargo* are entangled with the idea of *carrying* items. The entanglement begins with the Romans. Latin has the word *carrus* (wagon and also the source of the word *car*) which in Late Latin provided *carricare* "to load a wagon" and *cargar* "to load or impose taxes". Many taxpayers can empathise with the idea of taxes being a heavy wagonload of a burden to carry. By the time the word arrived in Spanish as *cargo* it meant burden. Finally in the 1650s *cargo* crept into English as "freight loaded on a ship".

Cargo cult entered English in 1949 when several small South Pacific tribal societies were found to have established religions based on *cargo* from Western ships. The islanders didn't understand how manufactured goods such as radios were made or how they worked. They made imitations using their own resources but these didn't work in the same way. Their rituals presumed the *cargo* was made by their deities.

Their aim was to ensure the cult members had more such items.

Cargo pants entered English in 1977. These loose fitting casual trousers with large pockets on the thighs were named after the *cargo pocket* (1944) - originally a feature of military trousers.

Cockpit

A *cockpit* is more commonly used as an aviation term since 1914 and even in racing cars, but it originated along with other flight terms like *pilot*, *crew*, and *rudder*, on ships.

The space below the lower gun-deck served many purposes. In quiet times it was the midshipman's mess, but in times of battle it was the surgeon's operating room.

Such a space would have been blood-splattered and reminded the crew in the 1600s of a similar space ashore where trained fighting birds would battle to the death, the *cockpit*.

The name stuck with the advent of yachting where a similar spot often houses the navigational and steering gear.

Crow's Nest

The *crow's nest* is a small platform near the top of a mast where a lookout could perch looking for land or the sails of another ship. Not all *crow's nests* had a railing or enclosure so being the lookout could be a tricky job, particularly in rough seas or high winds. As the rolling of the ship was amplified by the height of the mast any sailor sent to the *crow's nest* was considered to be on punishment as even experienced sailors would experience severe sea-sickness in that position.

The *crow's nest* may have been invented by the arctic explorer William Scoresby in 1807 when he lashed a barrel into position.

Legend associates the term *crow's nest* with the Vikings who carried crows or ravens on their ships, sometimes in cages lashed to the mast. When visibility was poor they would release one of the birds and follow its course as it would fly straight for the nearest land. If the crow returned it wasn't able to find land.

Sadly this story is unlikely to be true. The elevated structure is more likely to have reminded the sailors of the large *nests* crows build high in tree tops, close to the trunk.

However the same practice was used in British coastal ships in a later era with a cage of crows carried aboard for use when the helm was unsure of their bearing or in foggy weather. All sailors knew the bird would head for land *as straight as the crow flies* thus giving rise to that expression.

The lookout in the *crow's nest* sighted the New World before Christopher Columbus.

Deck

The *deck* is the floor of the ship, and a ship may have more than one going down into the hull. *Deck* is also used in various shoreside expressions like *hit the deck* (drop to the ground), *all hands on deck* (everybody gather round), and *I'll deck him* (I'll punch him) most of which originated afloat.

Deck entered English around 1450 from *dekke* which meant a covering extending from side to side of a ship. Essentially a *dekke* was a form of awning to keep sun or rain off sailors in an open hulled boat. It only later evolved into a solid plank floor to serve the same purpose. *Dekke* came from *dec* and *decke* in Middle Dutch and ultimately from the Proto-Germanic word *thakam* (to cover). *Thakam* is a source for *thatch* too. It's that idea of covering that also gives us the idea of *decking* or *bedecking* a room with decorations (*deck the halls with boughs of holly*, for example).

Deck has given modern English more than phrases however. The idea of a *deck of cards* arose in the 1590s perhaps because the cards were stacked like *decks* in a ship. A *tape-deck* (1949) comes from the flat surface of old reel-to-reel tape recorders and probably explains the term for a DJ's *turntable deck* as well.

You might guess the useful garden *deck chair* (1844) had a nautical origin, and you'd be right. They were first used on ocean liners.

Being *on deck* was in nautical use by 1740 to indicate crew being ready for duty but by 1852 was being used to indicate the batter in baseball was ready at the plate. *To clear the deck* dates back to 1852 and comes from the idea of preparing a ship's *deck* area for action.

One less obvious link is to public transport buses, the ones with two floors in particular. The word *double-decker* was first used to describe ships with two *decks* above the water line (1835) and only later used to describe the two-tiered buses (1867) on dry land.

Galley

Galley is one of those words with a multitude of uses on a ship and on dry land. The *galley* on a boat is the kitchen area and is typically neat and full of clever storage ideas.

Its space-saving design gives us the concept ashore of a *galley* kitchen, one that makes ingenious use of limited space. For the same reason the food area on a plane is called the *galley* too.

In publishing, a *galley* is another term for an ARC (advance review copy) or proof copy – an early copy designed for book reviewers or proofreaders. The *galley* was an oblong tray that held the type once it was set (probably looking a little like the shallow *galley* ship) and it entered English in the 1650s with the idea of a *galley* proof following in the 1890s and is still used today, for example Net Galley, the book review website.

Galley entered English in the 1200s from the Greek word *galea* via Latin and Old French. The ship came first, with the cooking association arising around 1750.

Gangplank / Gangway

A *gangplank* is a board or ramp used as a removable footway between ship and shore. It's also called a *gangway*.

Gangplank entered American English in 1842 and in doing so replaced the earlier term of *gang-board*. The idea of *gang* as a "path or passage for walking" has strong nautical links but my theory is that it came from the Scots.

Scotland's most famous poet, Robert Burns, had many quotable lines but one of the most popular is from his 1785 poem "To A Mouse" which contains the following line -

> *The best-laid schemes o' mice an' men*
> *Gang aft agley*

Which translates as

> *The best-laid plans of mice and men*
> *Often go astray*

Gang means go. It is conceivable that it contributed to the origin of *gangway* and *gangplank*.

Fender

A *fender* is an object hung over the side of a ship to protect the hull from collision with a pier. *Fender* is actually a shortening of *defender*, and entered English in the 1200s.

Fender ventured landward in the 1600s as part of a fireplace setup and later transferred in the *defender* role to cars in the 1920s. A *fender-bender* being a low impact car crash emerged in the 1950s.

Figurehead

The *figurehead* on a ship is a carved wooden figure attached to the front of the ship. You might conclude that a *figurehead* in a business or political setting also has a wooden block for brains, but that would be entirely your own affair.

The design of a *figurehead* is often related to the function of the ship it adorns. *Figureheads* can be male or female and often were associated with bringing good luck to the ship.

Adornment of the prow of ships goes back to antiquity – eyes on Greek and Phoenician galleys, holy birds on Egyptian boats, carvings of deities on Roman galleys, toothy large-eyed carvings on Viking longships etc. More elaborate carvings began in the 1500s. In a world where many couldn't read, the uniqu*e figurehead* identified the ship.

Mermaids were frequent subjects for *figureheads* thanks to superstitions around women on board vessels. Women were terribly bad luck in general and caused bad weather, but bare-chested women were fine. Luckily mermaids were always depicted without a top, so they bared their bodies on the *figurehead* to appease the sea gods and nature into staying calm.

The crew were often very fond of their ship's *figurehead*. They tied a hammock across the eyes of the *figurehead* on the *Royal George* so it wouldn't have to see a humiliating retreat and when the figurehead on the *Brunswick* had its hat blown off the captain donated his own as a substitute.

Fo'c'sle (forecastle)

Sailors were addicted to dropping and adding letters to commonly used words. You couldn't be on shore, you were ashore. You'd be afloat rather than floating. The boatswain became the bo'sun. Perhaps the most extreme of these which survives today is *forecastle* which is now *fo'c'sle* and is said as folk-sill and again marks a landlubber from a salty old sea dog, or is that an old s'dg?

The *forecastle* is the section of the upper deck at the bow, but forward of the foremast, or in landlubber terms – the front bit of the deck.

Foghorn

Describing a sound or person as being like a *foghorn* is rarely a compliment. *Foghorns* are designed to be loud warning sirens to advise of unseen obstacles, especially in coastal locations. Growing up on the coast, I learned how to sleep through foghorn calls. Like many around Ireland I miss them since the Commissioners for Irish Lights decided to discontinue their use in 2010 because of the increased usage of GPS and Doppler RADAR by shipping.

Foghorn is a compound word of *fog* and *horn*. *Fog* entered English in the 1500s to describe thick, obscuring mist from a Scandinavian source such as *fog* in Danish (spray, shower, or snowdrift) or Norse *fjuk* (a drifting snowstorm). The idea of being *in a fog* as a way of describing being lost and unable to decide what to do arose in English in the 1600s.

One particularly loudmouthed character to be named after this piece of ship equipment is *Foghorn Leghorn*, the drawling Looney Tunes rooster created by Robert McKimson in 1946 and originally voiced by Mel Blanc.

Gaff & Gaffe

A *gaff* is a boat hook. It snuck into English in the 1300s from the Old French word *gaffe* (same meaning).

By the 1800s *gaff* was a Scottish word to describe rude or loud talk and shortly thereafter it was being used in English slang for a fair, cheap music hall, or place of entertainment. This is probably the version which has entered urban slang in the phrase *"free gaff"* to announce a dwelling without parents present, and hence particularly attractive to teens.

By the early 1900s the associated word *gaffe* had arisen to describe a clumsy remark or blunder, again from the source word *gaffe* in Old French. It's hard to tell if the link occurred in French or in English but *gaffe* and *gaff* are definitely linguistic cousins.

Grapnel

A *grapnel* is a light anchor with very sharp flukes. Attached to a rope the *grapnel* could be thrown at a target ship to aid sailors in boarding her, or pulling her closer. You may well have seen them featured in spy and adventure movies as a way for the protagonist to climb a wall.

Grapnel entered English in the late 1300s and is likely to come from the Anglo-French word *grapon* (a small hook), from the Old French *grapin* (hook). The same origins give us *grapple*, from the 1520s, and *grappling hook* for both seizing ships or persons.

Gunwale

This part of a ship is a trap for the unwary when it comes to pronunciation. Say it as gun-whale and you've marked yourself forever as a landlubber. The correct way is gun-ell. The spelling is sometimes adapted to gunn'l.

The *gunwale* is the elevated side edges of a ship which both strengthens its structure and provides a safety railing around the gun deck. On a warship the *gunwale* is pierced with openings to allow heavy guns and cannon.

To be *loaded to the gunwales* (i.e. to the top of the boat's hull) is to be quite drunk.

In the 1400s the *gunwales* were called *gonne walles* as they restrained guns on the decks from washing away in rough weather. A *wale* wasn't related to a brick wall on land but rather was an upright piece of timber on the side of a vessel.

Halyard

A *halyard* is a rope used for raising or lowering a sail and it's been part of nautical English since the 1600s but was originally spelled as *halier* (in the late 1300s). *Halier* was also a carrier or porter so the meaning of *hauling* was there from the start. The change in spelling probably came about because of the logical link to a *yard*, a beam that supports a sail. So *halyard* was literally a *haul-yard*.

If you're walking near sailing boats and can hear rigging pinging and rattling off metal masts, those are probably *halyards* you can hear.

Hammock

This bed, made from rope mesh or canvas and suspended at both ends, is the poster child for summer lazy days, but it wasn't always so.

Hammocks come from Central and South America originally. The locals wove them from the bark of the *hamack* tree and discovered that sleeping above ground level reduced the amount of bites from insects and animals. The man responsible for the spread of *hammocks* to Europe is Christopher Columbus. He brought back several in 1492 from the Bahamas to Spain.

Sailors soon realised the *hammock* was better than sleeping on a hard, dirty deck. They made the most of the available space and could be stored during the day. The *hammock* swung with the motion of the ship and occupants wouldn't fall out during rough seas as they might from bunks. If a sailor died and was to be buried at sea, their body was sewn into their *hammock* as a shroud with a cannon ball at their feet. The final stitch was through the nose of the corpse to ensure it was truly dead.

Hammock entered English in the 1650s from the Spanish word *hamaca* which originated in Arwackan (Haiti) and perhaps ultimately from Yukana *hamaca* and Taino *amaca*.

During the Apollo missions the lunar module was equipped with *hammocks* for the commander and lunar pilot to sleep in between moonwalks.

Hatch

When you compare a ship's *hatch* with *hatching* an egg the link isn't clear until you realise both relate to something opening.

A ship's *hatch* is defined as a small opening in a wall, floor, or roof to allow access from one area to another. *Hatches* on ships and submarines also appear ashore – ever hear of a *hatchback* car or an escape *hatch*?

Hatch as an opening in a ship's deck is first recorded in the mid 1200s and it took until 1931 to give us the related drinking phrase *down the hatch*.

Hatch comes from Middle High German *heck* and Dutch *hek* which both mean fence or gate. *Hatch* entered Old English as *haec* with the same meaning so a hatch was never quite a door but definitely was something that could open. The word *hatch*, in relation to baby birds, comes from German too, but a different root word.

To *batten down the hatches* is a phrase meaning to prepare for trouble. This was a physical preparation on sailing ships when the grille-like *hatches* to allow ventilation and light to the lower decks would let in water in rough seas. To prevent this the order *to batten down the hatches* would be given in advance of changing weather. The deckhands would then cover the closed *hatches* with tarpaulins. That covering was then edged with wooden strips known as *battens* to stop the tarps from blowing off.

Head

The *head* on a ship is the bathroom.

Roman galley ships had carved *heads* fixed on the bow, sometimes with fierce bronze beaks used for ramming other ships. The bow of a ship is sometimes called the *head* of the ship, for this reason.

As ship designs changed the *beakhead* was a work platform projecting from the bowsprit at the front of the ship which was decked with grating and hence open to the sea below. The constant rushing water made the spot an ideal, if rather public, lavatory.

Head has a myriad of meanings but one may be relevant. The source of a river is called the *head*.

Hull

This word for the body of the ship came from land to sea but in a charming fashion. *Hull* entered English in the 1550s. It is likely to have come from the similarity between the keel and the shape of an open pea pod, which gives an additional layer of meaning to the Edward Lear poem about the owl and pussy cat going to sea in a beautiful pea green boat.

In Latin a *hull* is *carina* (shell of a nut). In Greek you find *phaselus* for a light passenger ship or bean pod, and in French you'll discover *coque* for *hull,* walnut shell, or egg shell. It appears that observers have been comparing *hulls* to foods for many centuries.

Keel

The *keel* is the bottom of a ship's hull and it also describes the main timber, typically set in the lowest position and key to the construction of the hull.

Keel entered English in the 1300s probably from Vikings because it's found in Old Norse *kjölr,* Danish kjøl, and in Swedish *köl.*

Keel is sometimes used to describe specific flat-bottomed barge boats and this is what gets us the expression *on an even keel* to describe stability.

To turn a boat *keel* side up for maintenance (or in accidental capsizing) is what gives us the idea of *keeling over* in a sudden collapse (from the 1800s).

See also *keelhaul* in the Running a Tight Ship chapter.

Lifeline

Lifelines were ropes left trailing from the sides and rigging of sailing ships so if someone fell overboard or from the yards, they might be able to grab them and save themselves. It's a compound word in use since 1700 and modern yachts still feature *lifelines* to prevent sailors falling overboard.

The popular quiz "Who Wants to be Millionaire?" introduced the concept of *lifelines* for competitors who could phone a friend for help.

Line

A *line* is any small rope on a ship such as *cluelines, buntlines, bowlines, ratlines, marlines, lifelines*, etc.

Line originates with the Latin for *linen* cord (*linea restis*) and was first used in English (late 1300s) with regard to building work rather than sailing.

Log

A *log* is a piece of wood, but a *log* in the sense of a *ship's log* is something else entirely, although it's still related to wood. *Log* is a shortening of *log-book* dating to the 1600s. The *log-book* was a daily record of a ship's progress.

To measure the ship's speed a sailor lowered a physical *log* attached to a line from the side of the ship to the water. The line had knots, or coloured rags, knotted in at regular intervals allowing a counting of how quickly the *log line* was let out as the ship moved forward. This count was recorded as the speed of knots the ship was making at that time.

The ship's *log-book* might also record weather observations, crew issues, ports of call etc.

According to "Star Trek" ships' *logs* are still kept in future space travel. Certainly the concept of *logging in* found its way into modern computing, from as early as 1963. When a new user enters their password to use the machine this is *logged* in the *computer's log*. When the user is finished they *log off*.

Mainstay

The *mainstay* (late 1400s, compound word of *main* and *stay*) is the supporting framework for the *main* mast of a sailing ship. It also applies to the *main* ropes securing the mast in position. Since 1787, *mainstay* has come to mean the *main* support of any person or organisation, an indispensable colleague.

Mast

The tall poles in the centre of a ship from which the sails are rigged are known as *masts*. Ships may have no *masts* or up to five. On a ship with five *masts* they would be named as follows – the tallest is the *mainmast*, the second tallest is the *foremast*, the third tallest is the *mizzenmast*. After that comes the *jiggermast* and there's no standard name for the fifth but you may find a *spanker mast* on a barque, schooner, or barquentine.

The *masts* are then sub-divided from bottom to top as lower, *topmast*, *topgallant mast*, and *royal mast* (optional). The terms for all the parts were necessary to rule out confusion over which sails to set.

The word *mast* entered Old English as *maest* from a Proto-Germanic source word *mastaz* which also gives us *mastr* in Old Norse, *maste* in Middle Dutch, *mast* in Danish, and *maide* (stick) in Irish.

On a *single-masted* ship the *mast* was the dividing point between the officer and crew quarters which gives us the expression *before the mast* meaning "serving as an ordinary sailor".

Mizzenmast

The *mizzenmast* is the largest *mast* on a ship.

Despite being the *mast* at the rear of the ship the roots of the word *mizzen* all relate to the middle. *Mizzen* came into English in the early 1400s from Middle French *misaine* which in turn came from Old French *migenne*, Catalan *mitjana* and Latin *medianus* (of the middle).

Orlop

The *orlop* was the deck above the hold. It is a shortening of *overlap* (that which runs over the hold). On the *HMS Victory* (Lord Nelson's ship at the Battle of Trafalgar in 1805) the *orlop* was painted red to conceal bloodstains as the wounded were taken there to be treated by the ship's surgeon during battle.

Paddle

If your vessel is small enough you may move it by using a *paddle*. *Paddle* entered English around 1400 as *padell* to describe a small spade. It came from the Medieval Latin word *padela* which may have come from the Latin word *patella*, a little dish.

The shovel for digging on land didn't become a water-based tool until 1620 when it changed to describe a short oar with a wide blade, like a spade. The idea of using such a thing to beat clothes or people didn't arise until the 1800. The concept of *paddling your own canoe* came about in 1828.

There's also *paddle* as a verb, the idea of splashing about in the shallow water with your clothes held up. That use of *paddle* dates to the 1500s and appears to have come from German rather than Latin roots drawn from the verb *pad*, to take short steps, and the Low German *paddeln* – to tramp about, so we can conclude that the Germans gave us the pleasurable beach activity of *paddling*.

Painter

From the mid 1300s a *painter* was the rope or chain that holds an anchor to the ship's side. This came from Old French *peintor* and Latin *pendere* (to hang) and the root word *pen* (to draw, stretch or spin).

The idea of a *painter* as somebody who *paints* pictures enters English at nearly the same time and from the same linguistic roots.

Poop Deck

No, this is not where the sailors attended to calls of nature, that's the head. Nor is it where tired sailors slung their hammocks at the end of their watch because they were *pooped*. The *poop deck* is the highest deck at the stern of a large ship, generally above the captain's cabin. If there's a quarterdeck the *poop deck* will be above it. The captain would often direct battles from his high vantage point on the *poop deck*.

Poop deck entered English as a term for this area of a ship by the 1400s from Middle French *poupe* (stern of a ship) via Provençal and Italian and ultimately from Latin *puppis*. *Puppis* referred to the small sacred idol the Romans fixed to the stern of their ships to watch over them on the waters. Over time the word *puppis* referred to the entire stern.

Porthole

Porthole is a compounding of *port* and *hole* and entered English in the 1590s. *Portholes* come from Latin *porta* (door) via French *porte* (door) as they were more door than window at first.

The original *portholes* were wooden covers allowing cannons to be deployed on lower decks of ships rather than just on the main-deck in the open where the ship might become dangerously top heavy.

Propeller

Propellers are more commonly recognised as part of an airplane now but they started life on ships. The word *propeller* entered English in the late 1700s to describe ship's *propellers*.

A *propeller* is a fan which converts rotational motion into thrust power when a fluid (air or water) is moved over its shaped blades. Archimedes applied this to an irrigation screw, Leonardo da Vinci used a similar principle for his helicopter, and James Watt, the famous steam engineer, proposed spiral oars to *propel* boats in 1771. *Propellers* were initially fitted to submarines and later to ships, and eventually aircraft.

Propel entered English in the mid 1400s from Latin roots *propellere* (to push forward) from *pro* (forward) and *pellere* (push or drive).

Prow

The *prow* is the most forward part of the ship's bow which cuts through the water. Bow and *prow* are often used interchangeably.

Prow is used ashore for any jutting out aspect of a building or vehicle.

Prow entered English in the 1550s but it took a roundabout cruise from the Greek islands to England. The Greek word *proira* is the port of origin and it's related to *pro* (before or forward). Think of *pro*noun and noun if you need an example.

The next port is Latin and the word *prora*, after that it stops in Italian with *prua* although it's really Genoese. Genoa is famous as being the birthplace of Christopher Columbus and is still the most important Italian port. The city is known as the gateway to the sea. From Genoa the word set sail for Middle French with *proue* and by the 1550s it landed as *prow* in English.

Ratlines

Ratlines (1773) are the small ropes fastened to the shrouds (see below) to enable the crew to go aloft to trim and furl the sails. Sailors pronounce them as "ratt-lins". They were in use from the 1400s and were originally spelled *ratlings*, perhaps because of the sound of them in the wind.

Rudder & Rudderless

The *rudder* is a flat piece, hinged vertically, near the stern of a boat for steering. It is moved by using the *tiller* (see below) or ship's wheel. The same term is used for similar equipment on an airplane.

To find *rudder* in English you start with the Germanic root word *ro* (to steer) which gives us Old High German *ruodar* (oar), Dutch *roer*, Middle Dutch *roeder*, Middle Low German *roder*, Old English *rodor*, Middle English *rother,* and finally *rudder* in the mid 1400s.

To be *rudderless* is to flail around without any sense of direction, much as a boat without a *rudder* would flounder on the waves.

Scupper
{with thanks to Kimberly Sullivan}

The *scuppers* are the openings along the edges of a ship's deck that allows sea water to drain back to the sea rather than collecting on deck.

The origin of the word is somewhat confused but three good candidates exist. Old French *escopier* (to spit out), Dutch *schop* (shovel), and Middle English *scope* (scoop).

To have your plan *scuppered* is possibly related - your good ideas simply draining away, unused.

The expression *scupper that!* is said in frustration and means "throw that overboard".

Scuttle & Scuttlebutt

Butt is an old word for a barrel or cask. To *scuttle* something is to cut a hole in it – for example in the hull of a ship in order to sink it to prevent capture. A *scuttle* is also an old term for a porthole, again with the idea of cutting a hole in something, this time for light or access for cannons.

Scuttlebutt describes a cask or bucket with a lid. The lid had a hole in it so sailors could scoop out water using a drinking cup, but without allowing flies or dirt into the precious water supplies.

The *scuttlebutt* became a place to congregate and exchange news on ships from the 1700s, hence its modern meaning as gossip or insider news. It crossed over to landlubber use around the 1950s. The equivalent in an office ashore would be water-cooler gossip or the Australian furphy from World War Two.

Spar & Sparring

A *spar* on a ship is a wooden pole used as a mast, boom, gaff, sprit, yard, etc. The word comes from a wooden pole on land, typically a rafter, and dates from the early 1300s. It either came from a Proto-Germanic root word or Old French.

From the 1600s the idea of *sparring* entered cock-fighting, and by 1755 it had moved into boxing between humans. Some claim the idea of *sparring* as a casual form of fighting came from off-duty sailors playing (sometimes in earnest) with *spars*, trying to hit each other.

Starboard

Despite early navigation using the stars, the word *starboard* (for the right side of the vessel when facing the front) has nothing celestial about it.

Starboard entered Old English as *steorbord* and literally translated as *steer-board* – the side on which a vessel is steered. A *steor* was a rudder or steering paddle used to control the boat's direction.

The same concept is found in other Germanic languages of the time - *stjornbordi* in Old Norse, *stürbord* in Low German, and *stuurboord* in Dutch because all their boats were steered by a paddle on the right side. Similar words in French and Italian are loanwords from the Germanic languages.

The paddle being on the right led to the boat always being docked with its left side to the quay, ready for loading and this led to *larboard* (see the I Do Like To Be Beside the Seaside chapter).

The invention of the centreline rudder, brought to Europe by returning crusaders made the *starboard* steering paddle redundant and now boats can tie up on either the *starboard* or port side.

Steering Wheel

The *steering wheel* (1750), or ship's wheel, on a ship only gained common use in the early 1700s. The spoked wheel allowed the helmsman to turn and steer the vessel more easily than rudder or whipstaff systems.

This ship technology went directly into the development of motor vehicles.

The *steering wheel* also gives us expressions like *steer clear of* and *steering committee* (1887 in U.S. politics) which are all related to choosing the right direction.

Stern

The *stern* is the rear of the ship. The word (with this sense, not in the grim and forbidding sense which is entirely different unless you have an unhappy boat) entered English in the early 1200s from Old Norse *stjorn* which was a steering paddle set at the back of older ships.

Swab

A *swab* was a large mop, made from oddments of old rope, with a long handle. Sailors used it to clean the decks. A hand cleaning the decks with it was called a *swab* or *swabbie*. It was the lowest job on the ship and became a term of insult and common slang for a low-ranking seafarer.

The word *swab* came to English during the 1500s and has Germanic roots but probably arrived via the Dutch *zwabber* (mop).

The non-nautical *swab* for cleaning anything from a floor to your mouth which is used in surgery and hospitals arose from the 1800s.

Tackle

Tackle on board a ship refers to any gear on deck, but specifically blocks and their associated lines (as in *block and tackle*) which are used to raise and lower sails.

The word came to English from the mid 1200s Middle Dutch words *takel* (the rigging of a ship) and *taken* (to grasp or seize). The use of *tackle* to describe what you need for fishing arrived in the late 1300s and *tackling* in a sports sense is from 1876.

Tackle being used to harness a horse didn't arrive until the 1700s so this is one the sea gave to the land.

Tarpaulin

Sometimes shortened to *tarp*, this useful waterproof covering sheet has many uses ashore but it originated on ships.

Tarpaulins started life as hats. Seaman wore canvas hats that had been coated with *tar* to waterproof them. This was the standard approach for waterproofing in an era before plastic or technical fabrics. The hats were called *tarpaulins*.

In really bad weather they expanded this to capes. When it reached their britches they were called *tarry breeks* in the north of England. Sailors would apply *tar* to anything, including their plaited hair and this gave rise to the nickname *tar*, or *old tar*, to describe a sailor.

To *pall* something was to glut it, to fill it, in this case with *tar*. You saturated the cloth with *tar* to make a *tarpaulin*. The ship's longboat would have a canvas sheet treated in the same way and this is the use we're most familiar with now.

Tarpaulin was spelled differently in the 1600s as *tarpawlin* or *tarpawling*, but eventually settled to *tarpaulin* by the early 1700s.

Tiller

The *tiller* is a lever used to steer a vehicle, primarily on vessels although they were also used on early motorcars. The *tiller* is attached to a rudder post to provide torque to turn the rudder in the water. The *tiller* may be moved directly by the helmsman or via a ship's wheel.

In this particular case the land may have given the word to the sea, rather than the other way about. *Tiller* was used in the 1100s from Middle English to describe a twig. It appears to have migrated from there to describe somebody who *tills* the soil and grows crops, and only finally in the 1600s to define the wooden *tiller* on a boat, possibly from a tangent to the wooden stock of a crossbow.

Ton, Tonne, Tun

When burdened with a heavy load I often claim it weighs a *tonne* but I was never sure if the correct spelling was *ton* or *tonne*. Imagine my surprise to discover the answer when researching this book in the National Maritime Museum of Ireland (www.mariner.ie).

Tonne comes from the idea of a ship's *tonnage* but has little to do with the weight of the ship.

Tonnage, or as it was originally known *tunnage*, was measured for tax purposes and related to the number of *tuns* of wine the ship could carry. All good ships carry nothing but wine, of course.

One *tun* held 252 gallons of wine which is approximately 1,150 litres or 2,240 pounds of weight. So when I claimed my load weighed a *tonne*, I should have said *tun*.

The gross *tonnage* of a ship is the volume of its cargo space while the *deadweight tonnage* (commonly known as the DWT) refers not to "fifteen men on a dead man's chest, yo-ho-ho and a bottle of rum" but to the total weight of passengers, cargo, fuel, and stores minus the weight of the vessel herself.

As for the origin of *tun* as a word that has the fingerprints of many languages - Old English *tunne*, Old Frisian *tunne*, Middle Dutch *tonne*, Old High German *tunna*, German *tonne*, Latin *tunna*, Old French *tonne* and possibly even Middle Irish *tunna* and *toun* (meaning hide or skin, again something used to carry liquids). Words relating to ships often have a mongrel parentage like this, probably because sailors pilfered any word they needed to communicate and trade.

Topside

Topside is the compound word for the upper deck of a ship.

Topside has given us a type of shoe, the *top-sider,* in the 1930s. The *top-sider* is a casual footwear with grippy rubber sloes, perfect for a stroll on the upper decks. In the U.K. and Ireland the *top-sider* is better known as a deck shoe or boat shoe, for the same reasons.

Wardroom

This space on naval ships is the mess and lounge (dining and living room) for commissioned officers. Before 1700 officers ate in their own cramped quarters. The captain had his Great Cabin and under it was a space called the *wardrobe* where valuable items taken in battle were stored. The officers used it to hang their spare uniforms, when possible. Over time it became larger and gained use as a living space for the officers.

Windlass

A *windlass* is a winch which wraps a rope around a cylinder, especially on a boat or in a harbour. The winch itself has a land-based origin but the *windlass* has been linked to water throughout history.

Archimedes (died 212 B.C.), the Greek mathematician, inventor, and astronomer, invented the *windlass*. He's also the discoverer of the Archimedes Principle that a body immersed in water displaces an equal volume of water – a discovery popularly believed to have been made when he took a bath and rejoiced over his new idea with the exclamation "Eureka!"

Through history *windlasses* were used to lift heavy masonry in constructing stone buildings but they were also used for cocking crossbows, lifting water from wells, opening the lock gates on canals, and as an alternative to the capstan (discussed earlier in this chapter) in raising a ship's anchor.

Despite its Greek origins the word *windlass* appears to have Old Norse roots in English. Old Norse has *vindass* from *vind* (wind) and *ass* (pole or beam). This moved directly to Anglo-French *windas*, then to *wyndase* in the late 1200s and finally as *windlass* in English.

The town of Windsor in Berkshire, England is best known as site of Windsor Castle, a primary residence of the British Royal family. Its name in Old English (1036) was *Windlesoran* which translates as a bank or slope with a *windlass*.

2. Old Sea Dog Yarns

Yarn is associated almost exclusively with the idea of wool from sheep for the general reader now, although crafters will be aware of *yarn* spun from goat, possum, rabbit, and old t-shirts. The word root of *yarn* is related to animals but not to their fleece. It comes from an old root word *ghere* which means intestine, cut, or entrail. Not sure a sweater made from those would be a good thing. From there, *yarn* wound its way through Dutch, German, and Norse to reach Old English as *gearn*.

The idea of *spinning a yarn* reached print in 1812 with a nautical association of sailors engaged in sedentary work such as twisting together strands of old ropes to make to make twine or smaller ties for small jobs shipboard. The inclination of sailors was to tell a tale while doing such work and so the phrase arose. When the older hands recognised a tall tale was being told they'd accuse the teller of *spinning a yarn*.

However, this is one of those expressions that sailors probably borrowed from their wives and mothers on shore. *Spinning* fleece into yarn had been a female task for centuries and the women folk would be pretty good at telling tales while they worked too.

The rest of this chapter is filled with the tales those sailors told to gullible landlubbers when they returned from long journeys. In an era when most lived and died close to their birthplace, the sea dogs brought news of far flung exotic locations, unbelievable creatures, and inconceivably different cultures.

Atlantis, Hy Brasil, Tír na nÓg and other Mythical Islands

Old sea dog tales are awash with mysterious islands inhabited by strange creatures and likely to vanish if you look too hard. Whether these stories are prompted by over-consumption of grog is not for this chapter to decide but here's a selection.

Ogygia (pronounced Oh-gee-uh) is the mythical island home/exile of Calypso. In "Pirates of the Caribbean" Calypso is the rather angry goddess of the sea, but in Greek myths she is the daughter of the Titan called Atlas (yes the one that holds the heavens on his shoulders as punishment for defying Zeus). Odysseus stayed with her for a while during Homer's "Odyssey". Some think it's the island of Gozo in the Mediterranean.

Atlantis supposedly lies at the bottom of the Atlantic. It was probably invented around the time of Plato and even then wasn't treated as a factual location but used as a morality tale of citizens being punished by the gods for their sins when their city island is swallowed by the waves. A likely candidate to have prompted the tale is the Greek island of Santorini where, around 1600 B.C., a massive volcanic eruption and tsunami sank the Minoan town of Akrotiri.

The Irish one is *Tír na nÓg* (the Land of Youth) which features in many old stories. Every Irish child is taught the story of Oisin and *Tír na nÓg* in school. Again situated in the West (somewhere in the Atlantic) it was the sort of place you could live in, but if you visited

Ireland again and set foot on the ground, all your postponed years would catch up with you.

Another Irish one (possibly a variant of *Tír na nÓg*) was *Hy Brasil*. This land could be seen from Ireland on one day in every seven years, but otherwise was shrouded in mist. Anyone who's seen the many islands off the West coast will see how this could be true! It even appeared on many medieval maps. Despite the name, it has nothing to do with Brazil in South America.

The *Isles of the Blessed* or *Saint Brendan's Island* were other mysterious island(s) discovered by St. Brendan on his voyages around the Atlantic, this time off the coast of Africa. St. Brendan, also known as The Navigator, discovered America way before Columbus, or so we Irish like to claim. It has been proven that his type of boat could have made the trip he described, but we'll never know for sure.

His island again appeared on maps, including those used by Columbus, and the story went that he and his monks stayed five days while the rest of the crew back on the main boat saw the island disappear into mist for a year.

Some mythical islands in more modern times were the creations of famous authors. The continent of *Four Ecks* in Terry Pratchett's work bears a strange resemblance to Australia and J.R.R. Tolkien had his elves pass into the West to *Numenor*, a land of peace and perpetual youth akin to the legends of *Atlantis*.

Calenture
{With thanks to the late Terry Pratchett, "A Slip of the Keyboard"}

Calenture isn't a word in regular use, but the concept may be more familiar to you than the word itself. If you were in a desert and you suddenly spotted a city in the distance, even though you knew there was nothing there but more sand you'd be seeing a mirage. *Calenture* is similar but on the ocean.

Be-calmed sailors hallucinated fields around their motionless ships. They would then have to be restrained forcibly from diving overboard to enjoy the countryside. This delusion was often linked to a heat stroke or fever experienced by sailors in the tropics.

Calenture comes from Middle French *calenture* and before that from Spanish *calentura* which makes sense as the Spanish were early explorers of those oceans.

Modern medicine sees *calenture* as a psychopathological syndrome on long sea voyages rather than a fever. In the 1950s it was dismissed as mere heat stroke but sadly no Elizabethan era cures are recorded for the affliction, except perhaps returning to dry land.

Caul

A *caul* is the membrane surrounding a child before birth which contains the amniotic fluid. Sometimes a baby will be born still wrapped in it and legend had it that such a birth brought good luck. Children born like this were supposed to have the gift of eloquence and the *caul* was often kept by the families as it was believed to protect against drowning.

From Roman times and especially since the 1700s there was a lucrative trade in *cauls* with seafarers. This persisted for centuries. *Cauls* were listed for sale during World War One in newspaper advertisements as soldiers were particularly afraid of the danger of submarine attacks on troop ships.

Caul's word origins are unknown although later versions of the word were linked to cap or other forms of close fitting head gear in Latin, Italian, and French.

Halcyon Days

Halcyon days – famously calm and peaceful – are the legendary fourteen days of quiet weather at winter solstice when a mythical bird (possibly the sea and river bird, the kingfisher) was said to build its nest floating on tranquil seas. In classical mythology *Queen Halcyone*, the daughter of Aeolus (Greek God and Keeper of the Winds), when widowed threw herself into the sea and became a kingfisher.

English got the word *halcyon* in the 1540s from Latin *halcyon* and Greek *halkyon* which may be a misspelling of *alkyon* (kingfisher).

Dead kingfisher birds were hung up outside houses in France and Britain as weather vanes up to the 1900s – as apparently they changed direction when the weather was changing. This practice is referenced by William Shakespeare in "King Lear".

Knell

Where landlubbers have banshees wailing around a house (typically in Donegal where the wind howls in winter) to predict the death of somebody in the family within 24 hours, sailors have the seafaring equivalent, the *knell*.

This was a sound heard to predict a shipwreck. Unfortunately none of the stories describe the sound and the belief has faded over time so it's uncertain if *knells* still occur.

What is certain is that *knell* is also a term for the slow ringing of bell and was an Old English word *cnyll* so it has been with us for some time. There are similar words in Dutch, German, Swedish, Welsh, Danish, and Old Norse. *Knell* is often associated with the idea of a death bell, tolled to announce a death. It was a short hop to the idea of a sound predicting a death.

Leviathan

The land has its *behemoth*. You'll find it in the Book of Job in the Bible as a name for a massive animal. It may refer to a hippopotamus.

The sea has its *leviathan*, also thanks to the Bible. It's taken to mean a whale, a giant sea serpent, or possibly Satan.

The reality is nobody knows what animal these terms referred to. It's possible the poor creature has become extinct in the centuries since those passages were written but the next time someone says they have a *behemoth of a task* to perform ask them what sort of hippo they mean.

The next time a friend references *a leviathan of the deep* - ask them exactly what sort of whale they're talking about because some whales are actually pretty small. The dwarf sperm whale is the smallest, in case you're wondering, at two metres in length.

Leviathan entered English as a word in the late 1300s and by the 1600s was being used to mean something or somebody large or powerful. The word itself is from Late Latin *leviathan* which came from Hebrew *livyathan* – a dragon, serpent, or huge sea animal. Its roots may rest in *liwyah* (Hebrew for wreath, from the idea of coiling) or Arabic *lawa* (to bend or twist).

Odyssey

"The Odyssey" is an epic poem written by Homer in the 8th century B.C. and might perhaps be described as the original sailor's yarn. Set in the 13th century B.C. during the Bronze Age, the story tells of the Greek hero Odysseus who is sailing home with his men after winning the Trojan War. He is plagued by every form of obstacle you can imagine as their victory has irked the gods. His decade-long voyage brings him into contact with temptations, battles, and storms preventing him from reaching his faithful wife Penelope who is waiting patiently at home.

He has to overcome the one-eyed Cyclops, go literally to hell and back, be captured by Calypso, dodge cannibals, have his crew turned into pigs, avoid the lures of Sirens, and skip past the deadly whirlpool Charybdis. His homecoming doesn't go exactly to plan either.

The term *odyssey* has been used since the 1800s to indicate any long voyage or tough challenge.

Homer's poems are the oldest ones to have survived intact in Western civilisation and are still read and studied today.

Poseidon
(also see Neptune in the Eponyms chapter)

Poseidon was one of the major Greek gods, a fact which is unsurprising if you examine a map of Greece. Its aquatic territory is larger than its landmass. If the Greeks hadn't learned to handle boats, they would never have thrived as a nation. Placating the sea god was vital.

In Greek myth *Poseidon* was the son of Kronos and Rhea, making him brother to Zeus and Hades - one of the Big Three. After the Olympians defeated the Titans and Giants (no, not the sports teams, they came later) to gain control of the universe the three brothers drew lots to divide the world. Hades got "down below", Zeus the air and land of men, while *Poseidon* ruled the waves.

Poseidon built the walls of Troy as punishment for rebelling against his brother Zeus and he appears in Homer's tales of the Trojan War.

Like many of the Greek gods, *Poseidon* was a prolific father of offspring including – Pegasus, Orion the hunter, Cyclops, Charybdis the ship-eating monster who created whirlpools (see whirlpool in the Underwater chapter), and was indirectly responsible for the creation of the Minotaur.

Poseidon was also the god of earthquakes which he caused by banging his trademark trident on the ground. His favourite mode of transport wasn't a ship but a golden chariot pulled through the water by hippocampi – half-horse and half-serpent creatures of the deep.

Salt

Salt, a word which definitely comes directly from the sea, was once a taboo word for seafaring folk despite its vital role in preserving fish and the ironic fact that calling somebody *a salt* meant they were an experienced sailor.

One day in the early 1900s an Eyemouth fishing vessel ran short of salt and hailed a boat from Yarmouth. The Scottish captain called across that they needed something they couldn't speak about and the English captain, catching his meaning asked how much *salt* he needed.

He noticed the crew of the Scottish boat had disappeared below in an attempt to not hear the dreaded word. The reason for the taboo is supposed to be that if you asked for *salt* you might get too much of it in the form of a briny death.

Salt entered Old English as *sealt* from Proto-Germanic *saltom* which also provides the words for this seasoning in Norse, Saxon, Frisian, Gothic, Dutch, and German.

If you're curious about the legend of how the sea became *salty*, check out Whirlpool and Maelstrom in the Underwater chapter.

Sea Dogs

Sea lions and seahorses are real creatures, but *sea dogs* are something else entirely. Although *sea dog* may be a harbour seal, since the 1800s it is more often used to describe a sailor who has been at sea for a long time. From the 1600s a *sea dog* was a privateer or pirate. They were also sometimes called *sea wolves*, probably for their fierce predations on the waves.

Siren

A *siren* in modern English is a device which makes a loud signal or warning sound.

In Greek mythology the *sirens* were a group of women, or winged creatures, whose wonderful singing lured sailors to crash onto the rocks below them. Famously Odysseus tied himself to the mast of his ship to enjoy, and yet resist, their song while the rest of his crew blocked their ears and sailed past them safely.

The *sirens* were originally male and female but over time only the females survived in artistic depictions, mostly with wings or some bird-like attributes, possibly to link them to beautiful birdsong.

3. Underwater

Much of what a landlubber or even a sailor sees of the sea is the surface. It's easy to forget that the highest peak on Earth, Mauna Kea on the island of Hawaii, is mostly underwater and that when we talk about the deep blue sea we're not kidding. The deepest point (so far measured) on Earth is the Challenger Deep in the Mariana Trench. It's 36,070 feet (10,994m) deep. That's a mile more than Mount Everest's height. Many claim the greatest unexplored frontier remaining on our planet is under the sea.

In this chapter we take a look below the surface, exploring *scuba* and *submarines* along with words about the briny depths such as *whirlpool* and *groundswell* which despite the word ground contained in it actually relates to an underwater concept. The sea has even given us the words for monetary *currency* and electric *current*. So grab a *snorkel*, we're going in.

Barnacle

A *barnacle* is a small shellfish which lives on submerged wood such as ship hulls. *Barnacle* entered English as *bernak* in the early 1300s from Anglo Latin roots.

The *barnacle* confused early observers, especially its methods of reproduction. Up to the late 1600s it was believed that the *barnacle geese* (who migrate to the Arctic to have their young and then return to winter in Europe) hatched from *barnacle* shellfish. The crustacean's feathery stalks reminded observers of goose down feathers. One version even had the *barnacles* growing on trees, then dropping into the sea, and finally flying away as geese.

From the 1600s a *barnacle* was a term for a person who holds firmly to an office or position despite ability. It's used rarely now, but deserves a comeback.

The Bends & Decompress

The *bends* are the slang term for *caisson disease*, a medical condition first diagnosed when divers suffered during the construction of the foundations of Brooklyn Bridge in New York (1869-1893). It is also called decompression sickness and is a major peril for divers who surface too swiftly. The solo use of a *decompression* (hyperbaric) chamber to help the patient is where we get the idea (since 1964) of needing quiet time alone to *decompress* and relax.

A *caisson* is a large watertight chamber, open at the bottom, from which the water is excluded by air pressure. It is used in construction work underwater. Originally a *caisson* was a chest for moving ammunition, but this meaning is rarely used now.

The *bends*, despite the temptation to link them, are unrelated to any of the unproven theories around the origin of the expression *around the bend* to indicate mental unbalance.

Coral

Coral is the general name for the hard skeletons of various marine polyps. There are both warm water and cold water corals. Many of these organisms are still being discovered.

The word comes to English from Old French *coral*, Latin *corallium*, and Greek *korallian* which may in turn come from Hebrew *goral* (small pebble) or Arabic *garal* (small stone).

Coral also describes a particular shade of pinkish red from a specific *coral* found in the Mediterranean. The *coral snake* is named for its red stripes. *Coral reef* only entered English in 1745 as explorers ventured to more tropical locations.

Current & Currency

Ocean *currents* are the invisible power beneath the waves. They direct the movement of ocean water. They are influenced by the earth's rotation, the wind, the temperature, differences in salinity, the moon's gravity, and the depth contours of the shoreline and seabed. *Currents* can flow for thousands of kilometres and have huge effects on the climates of entire continents. Deep sea *currents* are called submarine rivers.

Current reached English from French in the late 1300s as *curraunt* (that which runs or flows) from Old French *corant* (running, lively) and Latin *currere* (to run).

This idea of something running being related to water flows from the 1500s. From the 1400s money was seen as *currency* because it ran from person to person. We get *current affairs* in 1776.

As early as the 1740s *current* was describing electricity running through a conducting body because electricity was presumed to be a fluid.

Drown

To be suffocated by immersion in water or other fluid. This concept entered the English language in the early 1300s but its linguistic origins are murky. It could have come from the Middle English *drunccen* (swallowed by water), or Old Norse *drukna* (be drowned) , but is most likely to trace its lineage back as far as Old English *drincan* (to drink).

The idea of *drowning* originally applied to ships as well as people.

Drowning is also now used figuratively ashore. For example, Sam was *drowning* in paperwork.

Ebb

An *ebb* tide is low tide or a falling tide. In Old English it was *ebba* and it came from German roots with various Germanic languages having related words – *Ebbe* (German), *eb* (Dutch), *ebbiunga* (Saxon), *ebba* (Frisian). *Ebb* can also be used a verb meaning to flow back or subside, for example, the sailor's enthusiasm for an early start *ebbed*, the more rum he drank.

It was once a widespread belief that births happened at the flow of the tide and deaths at the *ebb*. Parish records in coastal areas sometimes recorded the state of the tide at the time of death or birth. This idea was mentioned in the writings of Aristotle and Shakespeare's play "Henry V".

The *ebbs* and flows were also connected in fertility superstitions. A rising tide favoured the conception of a child. Farmer's wives thought that eggs brooded when the tide was going out would hatch as hens, whereas those brooded when the tide was coming in would hatch as roosters.

You can read more about tides in the Weather chapter.

Eddy

Eddy entered English in the 1400s from the Scottish word *ydy*, probably from the Old Norse word *ida*(whirlpool). As discussed in the entry for whirlpools (see below), maelstroms and eddies are a Viking tale and there's a particularly nasty example in Scottish waters.

Ida came from the Proto-Germanic term *ith* which means "for the second time" and contributes as a prefix to many Old English words such as those for reconciliation, restoration, renewal, rejuvenation, and finally *edwielle* - an *eddy*, vortex, or whirlpool.

Groundswell

Groundswell is most often used now in the phrase *groundswell of opinion*. That meaning dates to the early 1800s but the original *groundswell* was a broad, deep sea wave.

Ground in this context was the seabed and a *swell* was a wave. A *groundswell* was a deep ocean wave, triggered by a distant storm or earthquake, like a tsunami (see the Weather chapter). Such a wave often preceded the arrival of a significant storm, like a *groundswell of opinion*.

Periscope

A *periscope* is a mechanism to see above water when you're operating a submarine. The word dates to 1899 and is a compound of *peri* (around, from Greek) and *scope* (instrument for seeing, e.g. telescope, microscope, also from Greek). Its use of mirrors set at specific angles allows the user to see objects not in the direct line of sight. This was perfect for seeing from below in a submarine but also found use in World War I trenches, armoured vehicles, and in large crowds of people.

In 1430 Johannes Gutenberg (the printing press inventor) created a *periscope* for use at busy religious festivals, so the device predates submarine *periscopes* (1854) by many centuries.

Periscope is also the name of a video streaming app for those above water.

Ripple

A *ripple* is a very small wave and has been in English since the 1700s, originally to describe fabric folds.

Ripple joined the world of ice cream in 1939 when some genius streaked ice cream with coloured syrup in a wave pattern.

The idea of a *ripple effect*, especially in business and politics, is akin to that achieved by dropping a pebble in water, and dates to the 1950s.

Scuba

Scuba is actually an acronym as it stands for Self Contained Underwater Breathing Apparatus and that's exactly what it is.

Diving gear up to World War II was bulky, heavy, and cumbersome. Divers were rare creatures, primarily working on building bridges and marine structures. With the arrival of war and submarines attacks, the need for a simpler method of diving became urgent.

Several inventors worked on methods of bringing air to the divers and dealing with expelled carbon dioxide. *SCUBA* was developed in the 1930s and patented by U.S. Major Christian J. Lambertsen in 1952.

The best known of the inventors working on solutions to breathing underwater was Jacques-Yves Cousteau (and his partner Émile Gagnan) who together created the first safe open-circuit *scuba* during the German occupation of France. They called it the Aqualung and patented it in 1945. Cousteau became the most famous underwater explorer of the century and his films, research, and books did much to allow landlubbers an insight into the vast underwater world.

Sink

Sink came into modern English from the Old English word *sincan* (to go under or subside). This came from the Proto-Germanic *senkwan* which provided similar words for the same idea in Old Saxon, Norse, Dutch, and German.

Sink or swim arrived as a phrase in the 1660s and *sink without trace* arose in World War I military slang.

The noun *sink* evolved from the verb in the 1400s as a place for wastewater and by the 1560s was a shallow bowl in a kitchen with a pipe to carry away wastewater. A *sink* in science is a place where heat or energy leaves a system and that has been used since 1855.

Snorkel

A *snorkel* was first used to bring air to humans underwater, but not to swimmers. The *snorkel* (1944) was originally an airshaft in a submarine and was called a *Schnorchel* from the German slang for nose or snort which is related to *schnarchen* (to snore). It was named like that because it resembled a nose in shape and made a snorting noise while in use.

The arrival of the curved tube used by swimmers to breathe underwater only arrived in 1951.

Submarine

Submarine entered English as a noun to describe a boat that travels underwater in 1899 thanks to the Irish inventor John Philip Holland. In the 1700s, submarine was an adjective to describe underwater sea creatures.

The abbreviated form *sub* was first used in 1917 and by 1955 it was a type of sandwich because of its shape.

Pig boat is the U.S. Navy slang for *submarines* because of the pungent aroma of their crews when they come ashore after a long posting.

Torpedo

A *torpedo* comes from the underwater sea to the dictionary, twice. The first *torpedo* (1520s) is an electric ray fish that produces an electric charge to stun prey and to protect itself from predators. Its name came from Latin *torpere* (be numb). The largest species grows to 200 pounds (91kg) and preys on small sharks. Its shocks are up to 220 volts. The ancient Greeks and Romans used torpedos in medicine, believing you could cure gout by standing on one or cure a headache by holding one to your temple.

The second *torpedo* (1776) was a floating explosive device, or mine, used to blow up ships. The self-propelling *torpedo* wasn't invented until 1900 and it was then that *torpedo* became a verb (to sink ships via *torpedo* attack).

The same Latin root gives us *torpid* – to feel numb and stupefied, like the effects of *torpedo* fish.

Wave

The sea wouldn't be the sea without *waves*. *Wave* entered Old English as *wagian* (to move to and fro) from Proto-Germanic *wag* long before *waves* relating to people arrived in 1852, *waves* in physics in 1832, *heat waves* in 1843, and *to make waves* in 1962.

There are various traditions around the world about which is the most dangerous or powerful *wave* at sea. Some say the third, others the seventh, and more say the ninth but despite the temptation to see patterns in the *waves*, the reality is that no particular numbered *wave* is more dangerous than the others. Having said that, you should always keep a weather eye for tsunamis (discussed in the Weather chapter).

Whirlpool & Maelstrom

A *whirlpool* is a quickly rotating mass of water in a river or sea into which objects may be drawn, usually caused by meeting currents. Other words for *whirlpool* are eddy (discussed above) and *maelstrom*.

Whirlpool is an Old English word (1520) compounded from *whirl* and *pool*, earlier spellings included *hwyrfepol* and *wirfelmere*.

Charybdis is perhaps the best known *whirlpool* in the world thanks to Homer's "Odyssey". That *whirlpool* is between the coast of Sicily and the Calabria region in Italy in an area of strong tidal currents.

The famous Austrian pastry, the *strudel* (1893), is named for *whirlpools* as *strudel* in German literally means eddy or *whirlpool*.

Maelstrom is used as a synonym for *whirlpool* and was originally the name for the strong tidal current moving past the Lofoten Islands in Norway, near the Arctic Circle. Various legends surrounded that particular place – either it was the entrance to hell or the mouth of a giant whale waiting to eat entire ships. When the wind and current are in opposing directions it poses a genuine threat to shipping and could sink a ship.

Maelstrom comes from Norwegian compounding of *male* (to grind or churn) and *strøm* (current).

The Norwegian *maelstrom* loaned another legend to one at Swilkie off the Scottish coast via Viking settlers. The resulting story explains why seawater is salty.

The King of Denmark owned a magic mill called Grotti which was tended by two strong women Fenia and Menia (Grotti Finnie and Grotti Minnie, witches in the Scottish version of the tale). They turned the millstones to make peace and prosperity but one day they were captured by a Viking who carried them off in his ship along with the mill. He ordered them to grind salt, a valuable product, and this they continued to do until the ship filled with salt and it sank. They continue at this task under the waves and that's why the sea is salty and the waves churn above the mill in a *maelstrom*.

The real reason the seas are salty can be explained with science. As water flows down rivers to the sea it picks up minerals from the land over which it passes. When that water evaporates from the seas (as part of the water cycle) the salt it contains is left behind. As time passes the sea water becomes more and more salty.

4. Crew

Boats may have only one crew-member (a kayak for example) but the old sailing ships had crews which might number in the hundreds. All those sails needed teams of sailors to hoist, reef, and furl if you wanted to get anywhere. The roles were varied and many came with their own special name, which have crept into the English dictionary.

The names for crew roles also yield information on class in the navy. The names of lower ranks - *bo'sun*, *coxswain*, and *seaman* - came from the people's language (Anglo Saxon) while the officers – *admiral*, *captain*, and *lieutenant* – all arrived via French, the language of the medieval English nobility.

One person also deserves a mention here, despite never being a crew-member, the *landlubber*.

A *landlubber* is a person unfamiliar with sea-faring ways. You'd think it came from land-lover but in fact *lubber* means clumsy. For a passenger new to a ship, and consequently without their sea-legs, clumsy would be a good descriptor. The term is, of course, an insult but sometimes used in an affectionate way.

Landlubber, or lubber, arrived in English during the 1300s and may have a Scandinavian origin from *lubber* (a plump, lazy fellow). It was also used in other contexts such as an *abbey-lubber* for a lazy monk (1500s), the mythical herb *lubberwort* which produced laziness, and *Lubberland* – an imaginary place of plenty without the need for work.

Admiral

Considering the popular idea that Arabia is a place of sand dunes, probably thanks to Hollywood, it is surprising to find that *admiral* has Arabic roots. It can be forgotten that the Arabic desert people learned sea-faring after the great expansion of Islam in the 600s.

Amir is the Arabic word for a Muslim chieftain. *Amir* appears as a loanword in several medieval Latin documents in various spellings – *amiratus*, *admirandus*, and *admirallus*. The added d to the later two is thanks to confusion with the Latin verb *admirai* (to admire) and even more confusion is thanks to the Arabic phrases *amir al-'ali* which means supreme commander and *amir-al-bahr* commander of the sea.

Using *admirallus* to describe the commander of a fleet began in Sicily in the 1100s, was adopted by the Genoese, and spread to western Europe until it landed in Middle English about 1200.

From 1400, *admiral* was used to denote the highest ranking naval officer.

Bosun

Sailors love to abbreviate. The *coxswain* becomes the *cox* (see below), forecastle becomes *fo'c'sle* (see the Parts Of Ship chapter), and the *boatswain* becomes the *bo's'un* or *bosun*.

The *bosun* is an experienced sailor who supervises the deck crew. On a merchant ship this is the petty officer in charge of hull maintenance and related work, while in the navy the *bosun* is a warrant officer in charge of the hull and related equipment.

Boatswain, the origin of bosun, is a simple compound word of *boat* and *swain. Swain* means servant and comes from the Old Norse word *sveinn* (a boy servant).

The *bosun* has the privilege of carrying a special silver *bosun's* whistle which they use to call hands to duty. Because of the whistle's high pitch its call could be heard even during high winds. Various commands were indicated by different notes, or combinations of notes – *haul, away boats, all hands on deck, pipe down, carry on,* etc.

Pipe down, now used by parents to children, was the routine naval order for silence and an end to the day. *Piping hot* was a signal when meals were served.

When an important visitor, or the captain, boarded the ship the *bosun* would use his whistle to alert the crew. This tradition, called *manning the side,* grew from the *bosun's* need to call crew to hoist visitors up the side of the vessel when weather was too rough for ladders.

The visitor would be hauled up, above crashing waves, in a *bosun's* chair. Modern *bosun's* chairs are similar to equipment used in rock climbing, complete with safety harnesses, clips and additional lines etc. but the original versions were improvised with a short plank or canvas for a seat and some clever knotwork by the sailors so the person could be pulled aboard from a smaller boat bobbing on the waves below. *Bosun's* chairs are still used today in ship painting, sea rescues, and window cleaning.

Thanks to Wordfoolery reader Rick Ellrod who reminded me that "Star Trek" featured an electronic *bosun's* whistle. Another case of that series using nautical history in a sci-fi context.

Captain (and Master)

A *captain* wasn't always the person in charge of the vessel. In medieval times the *captain* was an army officer or royal courtier who led his soldiers aboard to handle the fighting side of things. The *master* or bo'sun managed the crew and the actual sailing.

When, in Elizabethan times, voyages became longer the *captain* needed sailing knowledge too. Larger ships were commanded by *captains* while smaller ships had commanders or "lieutenants in charge". This explains Patrick O'Brian's wonderful seafaring book series about the "Master and Commander".

In the merchant navy the title *master* persists as he (or she) is concerned with ship handling rather than fighting.

Commodore

A *commodore* as a naval officer arrived in English in the 1690s either from Dutch *kommandeur* or French *commandeur*. It became a rank in the U.S. Navy in 1862 – above captain but below rear-admiral.

The *commodore* 64 was also a popular early personal computer during the 1980s. Introduced in 1982, it sold 17 million units and is listed in the Guinness World Records as the highest selling computer model of all time.

Coxswain

A *coxswain* is a totally different crew-member depending on boat type.

The *coxswain* in a small rowing boat with a team of racing rowers is the *cox*. The *cox* is the steersman and often the one shouting at them to pull harder or co-ordinating the rhythm of their stroke.

The poor *cox* (used from 1869), generally smaller than the rest of the crew, is often thrown into the water at the end of the race. The tradition of the toss is that only the *cox* of the winning team is thrown.

Winning *coxswains* delight in walking around soaking wet afterwards with a medal around their neck. Youth rowing teams love this particular tradition.

On a ship, the *coxswain* is in charge of the ship's boat and its crew.

The word *coxswain* is a compounding of two Middle English words – *cok* for a *cockboat* and *swain* which meant servant and which originated in Old Norse as *sveinn*, a boy servant. The two together gives us *cokswayne* and finally *coxswain* in English by the 1400s.

This leaves only the mystery of what a *cockboat* is. *Cock* is an obsolete Middle English word for a small boat which comes originally from the Latin word *codex* or *caudex* (a block of wood) via *coque* in Middle French, so

I can only assume a *cockboat* was a small wooden boat.

Crew & Crew-cut

Crew in modern slang is a group of friends who hang out together but the word has salty roots, as does *crew-cut*.

Crew comes from Latin originally, the verb *crescere* meaning to arise or grow. *Accrue* has the same source.

The idea of a *crew* being an additional number of people comes from an old, now obsolete word in Old French, *crue*, for additional soldiers sent as reinforcements around the mid-1400s.

By the 1690s the idea of *crew* revived and was associated with sailors of a ship's company and from there it crept into *crews* on airplanes (along with galley and pilot) and later in the friendship meaning.

What about *crew-cut* then? It dates to 1938 and was the preferred hairstyle of the boat *crews* at Harvard and Yale, before becoming more widely popular.

Galoot

When the wonderful Arthur Ransome (British author of the excellent Swallows and Amazons boating books for children) gave *galoot* to a character as her favourite slang word it cried out for investigation.

Galoot is nautical slang for an awkward or boorish man, specially a new recruit to a ship's crew. Originally it was used by sailors to indicate the crew member was a soldier aboard rather than a seafaring expert. It dates to about 1812 and may be linked to *galut* in Sierra Leone, a creole term for a galley slave.

Governor
{with thanks to zznewell on CritiqueCircle}

Governor isn't a crew member you would expect on board ship but it has watery roots nonetheless. The word *governor* entered English around 1300 as *gouernour* – a protector or guide and by the late 1300s it had changed to be one who *governs* or rules. The word came to English from Old French *governeor* – a prince, ruler, or helmsman.

French had borrowed the word directly from the Latin *gubernatorem* which was a director, ruler, or *governor* but it had an original meaning of steersman or pilot. The adjective form in English, *gubernatorial*, is a throwback to the Latin.

The ship's helm isn't called a *governor* anymore and luckily *governors* aren't asked to steer ships either.

Grommets & Idlers

Grommets weren't always small useful gadgets. They were ship's boys, apprentices who did menial tasks aboard. The name comes from Spanish *grumete* (a novice seaman) and the term was originally applied to boys from the *Cinque Ports* who tended the ship when she was in port.

The *Cinque Ports* (French for Five Ports) were a medieval group of ports in Southern England who furnished men and repairs to the British fleet, up to the time of the Spanish Armada when silting of the harbours limited their usefulness.

A useful junior sidekick certainly explains why Aardman named Wallace's loyal canine pal *Gromit* in the Oscar-winning animated Wallace & Gromit movies.

You might think that *idlers* would be the opposite of *grommets*. Nowadays an idler is someone who shirks work, but in original 1700s usage an *idler* was a crew-member who worked regular daytime hours on the ship - a carpenter (who often handled amputations because they had the saws), sail-maker, or surgeon - and hence was spared the night watches. They were idle during the night, hence *idlers*.

Gunner

It is debatable if the word *gunner* came from the army or the navy. The word entered English in the 1300s as *gonner* - somebody who operates a gun, or a catapult.

Shipboard the *gunner* was an important job. He led teams of 4-6 men in aiming guns from the pitching deck of his ship at the moving target of the enemy ship. The team for each cannon took care of loading, aiming, firing, resetting, and swabbing for each shot. The *gunner* checked the cannons weren't overheating (and hence liable to *burst their barrels*) or recoiling in a dangerous fashion. You really don't want to be behind a ship's cannon if it gets loose. The *gunner* also co-ordinated the timing of broadsides.

Helmsman & Helm

Helmsman dates to the 1620s and is, as you might expect, the sailor who operates the *helm*. Typically in a lifeboat crew the *helmsman* (or cox) is in charge of the lifeboat and navigation.

A *helm* can be two things. The first is a *helmet*, from the Old English word *helm* with roots in German, Norse, and various cousins in Saxon and Gothic. The second is the mechanism by which a ship is steered, from Old English *helma* with roots in German and Norse, specifically words denoting a handle or a grasp. The two words appear to be unrelated despite their similar periods and spellings.

The idea of the *helm* being a handle makes a great deal of sense when you consider early ship steering techniques. The *helm* was, before the advent of the ship's wheel, a large handle which turned the rudder in the water, thus influencing the direction of travel. The job of the *helmsman* is to take the *helm* and steer the ship.

The concept of taking the *helm* of a project and steering it to completion has become common ashore.

Longshoreman & Stevedore

A *longshoreman* is one whose work is to load/unload cargo from ships. It's an American English word dating to the early 1800s and is a shortening of *alongshore*, i.e. a person who works *along the shore*.

Stevedore is used in British English for the same work and again dates to the 1800s and is an adaptation from the earlier 1700s word *stowadore*. This came from the Spanish word *estibador* "one who loads cargo, a wool packer" which comes from Latin *stipare* "to pack down or press".

Mate

The role of *mate* aboard ship has moved on considerably since pirate tales opened with dialogue like "Ahoy there, *mateys*!"

The *first mate*, also called the deck officer, acts as a captain's second-in-command. On smaller vessels the *first mate* is responsible for navigation and safety while on larger vessels with *second mates*, the *first mate* is in charge of passengers and cargo. *Mates* typically work their way up from deck crew or train in merchant marine academies.

Mate entered English from Middle Low German around 1350 with the meaning of comrade or associate from the same source as companion which comes from one you eat bread with, literally a *mess mate*. By 1450 *mate* described a companion on a ship. It didn't indicate a romantic link until 1540.

The idea of a *first mate* being second to the captain does make sense with the idea of friendship as the officers would eat together and often be friendlier with each other, rather than mixing socially with the general deckhands.

Nipper

There are two possible sources for the word *nipper* to describe a child – one afloat and one ashore. The nautical one seems slightly more likely.

The nautical origin relates to the anchor cable on large sailing ships, probably in the 1700s. The anchor rope was sometimes too large to fit snugly around a capstan on the quayside so smaller lines (called messengers) were used to heave the cable into position. These lines were *nipped* by the smallest crew-members, boys and young men with dextrous, small hands. They became known as *nippers* and hence youngsters on ship, and later on shore, were called *nippers*.

On land a *nipper* was also a child, but in this case a child pickpocket who pinched other people's property (1859 but possibly from 1530s), or as a youthful assistant to a carter.

Nipper is still used to describe children, particularly in British English and Irish English.

Petty Officer

The rank of *petty officer* (1570s) persists to this day, where it's roughly equivalent to sergeant or corporal in the army but they date back to the Age of Sail. The *petty officer* then would dress respectably and be a low-ranked officer but nonetheless had permission to walk the quarterdeck with commissioned officers.

Petty in this case comes from the French word *petit* (small) and it wasn't used in a negative sense at that time. You will also find *petty* as a synonym for small in *petty cash*, and *petty* used as an adjective for small-minded.

The northern lights were once called *petty dancers*.

Pilot

Pilot (1510s) is another word the sea has given to the air. *Pilots* were steering ships long before they were flying airplanes.

A *pilot* as one who steers a ship came from Greek roots. Greek *pedon* (steering oar) gave us *pedotes* (rudder, helmsman) in Medieval Greek, then *pedoto* in Old Italian, *piloto* in Italian, *pillote* in Middle French, and finally *pilot* in English.

Pilot moved from ships to the air with balloons in 1848 and thence to airplanes in 1907.

Other uses of *pilot* all relate to leading the way. We have *pilot episodes*, *pilot lights*, and even *pilot fish* (1630s) who were believed to guide sharks to their prey.

Purser

A *purser* on a modern ship, especially cruise ships, is in charge of finances and administration tasks. They communicate with crew and passengers. The *purser* on an airplane is the chief of the cabin crew and ensures all safety procedures are followed. Both roles spring from the *purser* on sailing ships.

The sailing *purser* controlled the ship's *purse* or finances. From the mid 1400s they managed the accounts and provisions.

The name came from *purse*, a Middle English word coming from Old English *pursa* (a little leather bag), Latin *bursa*, and Greek *byrsa* (leather). It's possible that the change from b to p as the leading letter was influenced by the Old Norse word *posi* (bag).

The idea of *pursing* your lips (1600s) comes from the drawstring closure on these little leather money bags.

Quartermaster

A *quartermaster* may be a landlubber or a seafarer. In military (and scouting) life they provided accommodation , transport, and supplies for troops. In naval life the *quartermaster* is a petty officer for signals and navigation apparatus.

Quartermaster entered English in the early 1400s as a subordinate officer whose duties included stowing cargo. From about 1600 the *quartermaster* organised quarters and rations for troops.

Quartermaster may come from the French naval term *quartier-maître*, Dutch *kwartier-meester*, or even from the German royal official the *Quartiermeister* who was the master of quarters or accommodation. Alternatively the term may come from *master of the quarterdeck*. The *quarterdeck* was where the captain and helmsman controlled the ship.

What *is* clear is that the navy got there before the army. The military *quartermaster* title came from the naval service.

On pirate ships the *quartermaster* was second only to the captain and he was usually elected by the crew. He could veto a captain's decision when the ship wasn't engaged in active battle or on a mission. He received a large portion of any booty. If the pirates captured a prize ship the *quartermaster* would often become captain of that ship.

The navy getting there first probably annoys *Q* considerably. The beloved gadget-dispensing character in the James Bond spy books by Ian Fleming and the popular movies is called *Q* for a perfectly good reason. The character is the *quartermaster*, hence the distribution of spying supplies, especially relating to navigation and signalling.

Skipper
{with thanks to Christine Byrne Carroll}

Everybody knows the *skipper* is the boss, on land and at sea.

Skipper is a much older word than you might guess, entering English in the 1300s. *Skipper* comes from Middle Dutch *scipper* from the word *scip* (ship) which also gave us ship.

A *skipper* can also be someone who *skips* (1400s) or a type of butterfly who appears to *skip* in flight (1817) but generally speaking the ship's *skipper* is too busy to *skip* on deck.

Waster

The *waist* of a ship is the centre of the bottom of the ship. This is typically where bilge water gathers. It's hard to pump out and stagnates to a filthy state. If enough lies there it affects the steering of the ship and needs to be cleared, a nasty job. Older, unfit, or pressed sailors, called *waisters*, would be given the task of clearing the *waist* of debris, water, and probably rodents.

Over time this changed to be *wasters* but remained associated with those who aren't able for tougher duties.

5. Sounds Fishy to Me

Across the vast oceans and along the wandering rivers of the world, one of the main interactions we humans have with the water that covers most of our planet is through fishing. Fishermen love to talk and their trade has contributed to the English dictionary.

Of course fishermen do sometimes exaggerate when talking about *the one that got away*. So it's unsurprising that this section includes *red herrings* and *hook, line, and sinker.*

Bait

Baiting a hook to attract a fish may be as old as time but *bait* has moved with the times. It's near impossible to avoid *clickbait* on the Internet and *jail-bait* is a frequently used term too.

Bait dates back to 1300s as an English word and is one the Vikings gave us. Proto-Germanic had *beita* as a verb meaning "to bite" and the Old Norse had *beita* as food, or *bait*, in particular for fish. It's not difficult to imagine Norse fishermen sharing the word with those on English or Norman shores.

The word *chum*, which means fish *bait* (*chum* as friend is different) usually formed from oddments of other fish, dates to 1857 and may come from the Scottish word *chum* which again means food.

Fluke

There are *flukes* on anchors and on whales so *fluke* and *fluky* both come from the sea. *Anchor flukes* (1560s), or possibly *fluke* fish, are the source.

The *fluke* fish's name entered Old English as *floc* from the Old Norse *floke* (flatfish) and *flok* in Proto-Germanic. In 1725 the whale's tail was named its *flukes* (always plural).

Then in 1857 *fluke* took a strange turn. A *fluke*, or *flook*, is defined as a lucky chance, specifically a luckily shot in the game of billiards (think pool or snooker and you're in the right area). This is tentatively related to the whale's ability to move quickly using its *flukes* (*to go a-fluking* is used in several sailing books of the period as a synonym for moving fast) just as a billiard player with a *fluke* shot will progress rapidly.

By 1867 to describe somebody or something as *fluky* was to say they depended on chance rather than skill, which seems unfair on the whales.

Gravlax

Gravlax is a popular Nordic dish of raw salmon cured in salt, sugar, and dill. The salmon is sliced thinly and usually served as a starter to a meal with dill and mustard sauce, either on bread or with boiled potatoes.

Gravlax is a compound Scandinavian word of *grave* (or gräva) and *lax* (salmon) – literally *grave fish*. *Grave* in this case relates to digging a trench in the ground and is linguistically related to a *grave* for burials.

The traditional method was to wrap the fish in birch bark and bury it where the wet cold conditions combined with lack of oxygen caused it to ferment but not rot. It used the bare minimum of salt, a valuable commodity, and preserved the fish for the long, cold winters.

The burial and fermentation is not part of modern *gravlax* recipes, to avoid food poisoning risks.

Go Belly Up

If a company or person *goes belly up* they have failed or died. When referring to a company it is likely that they have declared themselves bankrupt or insolvent.

Several dictionaries list the origin of this phrase to relate to how a dead fish floats on the surface of the water after death but further details are scarce.

Belly itself has old roots stretching back to Gothic *balgs* (wine skin), Old Norse *belgr* (bag, bellows) through Anglian and West Saxon to reach Old English as *belg*. All the versions referred to a bag, pouch, or even bellows and it was only in the 1100s that it started to be used as word for the stomach, particularly when associated with gluttony – a swollen stomach would appear to expand like a full bag or an air-filled bellows.

In the 1800s using the word *belly* was seen as impolite. Stomach, abdomen and tummy were used instead. The word was removed from many Victorian Bibles.

Hook, Line, and Sinker
{with thanks to Peter Sheehan}

To swallow a tall tale *hook, link, and sinker* originates in fishing. The three items are all vital pieces of tackle in angling – the *hook* to catch the fish, the *line* attached to the *hook*, and *sinker* weight to bring the *hook* down to the right level to catch the fish. A fish who takes all three is definitely caught and hasn't been wary enough of the bait.

The bait in the metaphorical sense is false information or a well spun, fake story.

This phrase appears first in print in American English during the 1800s but there was another phrase, also fishing related, used in earlier times – *to swallow a gudgeon* (*gudgeon* or dudgeon is a small fish used for baiting *hooks*).

Red Herring

A red herring is a false lead left by a writer of crime fiction, or a criminal, to divert attention from the truth, but *a red herring* is also a fish.

Herring is a white fish but when smoked for preservation it turns red and is then called a kipper or a *red herring*. In the 1680s there were references to *red herrings* being used by fugitives to obscure their trail as the bloodhounds used to track them were confused by their pungent aroma.

In 1805 the English journalist William Corbett wrote about using a *red herring* to mislead hounds following a trail during a fox hunt. He mentioned it in the context of the London press establishment publishing false accounts about Napoleon. Misleading news accounts are not a modern phenomenon.

The phrase got new use in the 1920s when American investment bankers used it to describe incomplete or misleading investment prospectuses.

Herring move in large shoals around coastal waters. They've been eaten as food since 3,000 B.C. and their valuable fisheries helped establish Amsterdam and Copenhagen.

On the Isle of Man, there's an old saying about the importance of the herring fishery - *no herring, no wedding*. If the fishing wasn't good there wouldn't be enough money to pay for a wedding.

The sheer size of the *herring* catch around Britain and Ireland in former times is hard to imagine. One town recorded a catch of four million *herring* in one season. In an era when everybody ate fish instead of meat during Lent, the importance of the *herrings* arriving offshore at various ports couldn't be overstated. Cheap and plentiful they provided regional jobs and food even during hard times right up to 1951 when the catch dropped so drastically that a ban was imposed on North Sea *herring* fishing.

Traditions around *herrings* abound. On Tyneside on Saint Agnes' Eve a young man who wished to know who he would marry would eat a raw *herring* whole. Whoever he dreamed of, if not kept awake with indigestion, would be his wife.

The word origin of *herring* is obscure with candidate words coming from Saxon and various Germanic languages. A strong possibility is *heri* in Old High

German which meant host or multitude in reference to the size of *herring* shoals.

In 1429 *The Battle of the Herrings* was fought at Rouvrai in France during the Hundred Years War in defence of an English convoy of provisions, some armaments but mostly *herrings* and other "lenten stuffe" as that Christian fasting period was approaching. The battle was part of the Siege of Orleans and was won by the English, who presumably celebrated by eating *herrings*.

Shark

The word *shark* entered English in the 1590s from unknown origins. A Captain John Hawkins brought a specimen back to London for exhibition. Although *sharks*, for example *basking sharks*, are present off the coast of the British Isles, the creatures appear to have been unknown in Northern Europe before then.

The word *sharker* for a dishonest person who preys on others appears in 1599. It may predate the naming of the marine animal.

Words for *shark* in other languages are very descriptive. In French you have *requin* (grimacer) and in Lithuanian it's *ryklys* (swallower).

A decade later *sharking* was a verb meaning to live by your wits. By 1707 a *shark* was another name for a pickpocket. Herman Melville (in "Mardi") said that sailors called brown *sharks* "sea attorneys" for their grasping natures. *Loan shark* arrived in the language in 1905.

There's also the idea of a *land-shark*, primarily in English spoken in Australia and New Zealand. A *land-*

shark is either one who speculates in real-estate (1800s) or one who preys on and cheats sailors on shore leave (1700s).

From the same roots we get *card shark* (*card sharp* is also correct, although less common), one who through skill or deception wins at poker and other card games. Cheating is not always implied.

Finally, in surfer speak, *sharks* are "men in grey suits".

6. Surfer Slang

While diving and snorkelling is covered in the Underwater chapter, there are, of course other water pursuits not requiring a boat. Surfing's popularity worldwide is huge and several pieces of its jargon have infiltrated the mainstream English dictionary. I've only included those in common use, but surf speak is fascinating, and very amusing, if you've time to kill online.

Coasteering and cliff diving have given us a couple of words too and are included here also.

Coasteering

This word has only recently arrived from the sea. It has one foot in the sea and one on the land.

Coasteering is a physical activity which combines sea swimming, climbing, scrambling, and cliff jumping along the coastline without the aid of boats or surfboards. The word first appears in 1973 but rose in popularity since the 1990s, particularly on the Welsh coast and has spread since then.

Cowabunga

This invented word was first used as an expression of surprise or anger by Chief Thunderthud in the "Howdy Doody Show", a television show for children broadcast from the 1940s to 1960s on NBC in America. The original spelling was *kowabonga*.

By the 1960s *cowabunga* was being used by surfers as a cry of triumph during elating moments on the waves. In the 1980s a quartet of (thankfully fictional) mutant turtles brought it to the mainstream, especially Michelangelo as it was his catchphrase.

The phrase continued in pop culture thanks to Bart Simpson, although he's more likely to say *"Aye, Carumba"* in the show.

Gnarly

Gnarly entered English in the 1600s to describe anything which is knotted and rugged, but is now more commonly used by surfers to describe particularly dangerous surfing conditions.

By the 1980s it had spread to general teen slang to describe something as either excellent or disgusting. This may be a little confusing for their parents, but that's the purpose of all teen slang.

Tombstoning

A *tombstone* is the marker for a grave, often with the person's name on it. It dates to the 1560s, or earlier and was originally the stone lid of a stone coffin. The city of *Tombstone* in Arizona, U.S.A. was founded by a prospector called Ed Schieffelin who was told his *tombstone* would be the only thing he would find there. He found silver.

Tombstoning as a verb is a diving term for dangerous diving into water from a particularly high place such as a cliff.

Tube & Tubular

Tubular is the adjective form of tube and dates to the 1670s. It describes anything shaped like a *tube* or pipe and comes from the Latin word *tubulus* (a small pipe). The Romans were very keen on indoor plumbing.

Tubular is also surfer slang, since the 1980s, for something being exceptionally good and hence akin to a *tube* (from 1960s) – a hollow curving wave which is ideal for surfing.

7. Sea Monsters

Examine an old sea chart and you'll find tentacled creatures lurking in the blank spaces. Ancient cartographers covered the gaps in their knowledge with imaginary lands or rumoured creatures from sailors who'd had a few tankards of grog too many.

This chapter will brave the depths and explore the more famous sea beasts, both real and imaginary. A few more common creatures have earned inclusion too, by reason of the strange sailing superstitions they inspired.

Cormorant

Since Roman times *cormorants* were regarded as harbingers of storms. In the first century B.C. Virgil wrote that when the cormorant birds were seen on land, rough weather would arrive at sea. This belief persisted well into the 1800s.

The cormorant is a large, black, seabird with a huge appetite which excels at diving for fish. Their name evolved from the Late Latin *corvus marinus* (sea raven) and they are sometimes called sea crows in the British Isles. When wet from the sea its head and dark wings gave it a bat like or devilish aspect in the minds of medieval observers who believed the Devil had leathery wings as well as horns. In John Milton's famous poem "Paradise Lost" (1667) the Devil is compared to a *cormorant* lurking on the Tree of Life and plotting there.

As a result *cormorants* were seen as ill omens and were sometimes killed on sight by landlubbers and sailors alike.

Fastitocalon & Jasconye

The *fastitocalon* is rarely mentioned in lists of sea monsters these days, but Saint Brendan saw one and he knew his salty beasts.

Saint Brendan, also known as Brendan the Navigator for allegedly discovering North America 800 years before Columbus, is a patron saint of mariners. One day, the story goes, he was looking out from the Scottish coast at Elachnave when he saw two monsters emerge from the depths, fighting each other. The weaker one called, in a human voice, on three Irish saints for aid – Saint Patrick, then Saint Brendan, and finally on Saint Brigid. After Brigid's name the attacker stopped and both monsters vanished beneath the waves.

Brendan later asked Saint Brigid why the sea creatures would respect her name so much and she modestly replied that while Brendan sometimes thought of worldly matters, she never did. Saint Brigid knew how to keep Saint Brendan in line.

It is likely he saw whales which were common along that coast at the time. Brendan had another whale encounter on his great Atlantic sea crossing when he and his monks moored at what they thought was an island, lit a fire to cook their meal and then discovered they'd tied up at a whale. The whale was calmed by the saint, who named him *Jasconye*, and it carried them part way on their journey.

A less friendly whale-like creature is the *Fastitocalon* who is a weed covered beast. *Fastitocalon* allowed unwary sailors treat him in the same fashion. Once they lit a fire he would dive to the deeps and take them all with him. *Fastitocalon* would be good friends with Moby Dick.

The *Fastitocalon* was described as a giant sea turtle in the earliest versions of this tale and that's how it got its name as it translates as tortoise shield in Greek. Later versions have the island being a whale and John Milton's epic poem "Paradise Lost" (1667) features the tale. It's a whale in his story but with some elements of Kraken legends entwined.

Kelpie

A *kelpie* or waterhorse was a dangerous water-dwelling beastie of Scotland. The Loss Ness monster is the most famous of the tribe. The *kelpie* appeared as a handsome man, or a horse, to tempt a woman with the plan of dragging them below the waters forever. They are recognisable by their hooves which can't be hidden even by fine clothes.

In some stories the *kelpie* keeps the human as their wife below the waves, constantly complaining of the damp. In others, the human becomes dinner and only the scraps of their entrails float to the surface. All end with the human never being seen above the waves again.

Usually a dangerous creature, the *kelpie* was also sometimes credited with keeping their mill-streams flowing for millers.

Kraken

Stories of the *kraken* have long been part of sailor-lore but only in recent times has the real life giant squid been discovered. Marks left by its suction cups on whales no doubt added spice to the tales in the past.

The *kraken* is most associated with Norway and that's where it gets its name. *Krake* there usually means a pole or post, but sometimes a crooked animal, or in this case a giant tentacled creature capable of snapping boats in two and dragging them to the depths.

Stories of the *kraken* are not confined to Norwegian waters, however. Homer included the Scylla in "The Odyssey" which strongly resembles the *Kraken* with its size and tentacles. Pliny describes them in his "Natural History" (77A.D.) as being common in the Mediterranean. Some theorists even claim the crew of the *Mary Celeste* were taken by one, although ergot poisoning seems more likely.

The discovery of the colossal squid (1981) which is even larger than the giant squid further explains the *kraken* tales, despite the fact that sucker marks found on sperm whales are more likely to come from the whale trying to consume the squid, rather than the other way round. The *kraken* needs a better publicist.

Mermaid

Mermaids are the best known legendary sea creature and their depictions in popular culture vary on a wide spectrum from adorable Ariel in Disney's version of Han Christian Andersen's "The Little Mermaid" to the predatory vampire-esque version in "Pirates of the Caribbean - On Stranger Tides".

Mermaid tales are amongst the oldest nautical stories. 6,000 years ago the Babylonians worshipped a fish-tailed god and the Syrians honoured a woman who was human from the waist up and fish from the waist down.

Later versions furnished the *mermaid* with bird qualities as well as fishy ones, but a connection with seals, in particular, persisted in many tellings. Often a *mermaid* would be persuaded to bear children for a human man and live ashore in human form but ultimately she would always return to the sea. Perhaps this was used as an excuse for broken marriages and runaway brides in the past?

Mermaids were always seen as sexual beings, able to tempt men. Mary Queen of Scots was represented as a *mermaid* during her lifetime, initially as a compliment, later in derision when her power faded.

Mermaids were symbols of vanity in Christian art, often found carved in medieval churches, perhaps as a warning to parishioners.

Mermaid became an English word in the mid 1300s spelled as *mermayde*. It was compounded from *mere*, the Middle English word for a lake or sea, and *maid*. Before that Old English had the idea of a *merewif* – a water witch.

In the 1660s you could order a *mermaid pie* which was a small pig baked whole in a pastry crust.

Nausea

Perhaps the most-feared of all sea monsters by landlubbers like myself, the dreaded *nausea* that comes with motion-sickness on boats, cars, and other vehicles has its roots with Greek seafarers. *Nausea* entered English in the early 1400s as a direct adoption from Latin but the Romans borrowed it from Ionic Greek *nausia* which literally meant ship-sickness as *naus* was the word for ship.

Octopus

An *octopus* may not be terribly monstrous today but they were fearsome creatures if you paid heed to sailors' stories in earlier times.

They were believed to be aggressive and dangerous, holding swimmers underwater and capable of downing ships. Victor Hugo, amongst others, wrote of them battling humans in giant form and called them devil fish.

The largest known *octopus* is the *giant Pacific octopus* and it can grow up to 20-30 feet in arm span (tentacle span?). Descriptions of larger animals are likely to be mis-identified colossal squid which can grow up to 60 feet in arm span. It is extremely rare that an *octopus*, of any size, would take on a human but some authenticated cases have been recorded.

Octopus became an English word in print in 1758. It describes the eight-armed cephalopod mollusks. The English word comes direct from Greek *oktopous* which is a compounding of *okto* (eight) and *pous* (foot).

The correct plural of *octopus* is not *octopi*. The proper plural is *octopodes*, although *octopuses* works better in English.

Pig

Pigs aren't scary monsters to landlubbers but they scared the wits out of some seafaring folk.

Seeing one was believed to be a bad omen for fishing or a voyage. They were never to be eaten or mentioned on board a ship. A sailor couldn't go to sea after seeing one, until the tide had ebbed and flowed at least once to take the bad luck away.

Sailors might call them beast, brute or curly tail, but never swine or *pig*. If they said *pig* by accident they had to say "cold iron" at once and try to touch some. Tradition held that touching cold iron, for example a horseshoe, would remove evil enchantments.

Mentioning pork on board was sure to bring a storm and certain gospel stories mentioning them were avoided in the local church. The Bible may be the source of the superstition, thanks to the tale of the demons driven out by Jesus into a herd of swine who then plunged over a cliff. The association of *long pig* with human cannibalism probably didn't help either.

Pig came from the Old English word *picg*, whose origins are unknown. Young *pigs* were called *pigs*, whereas adult specimens were *swine*. Calling a person (hopefully not a sailor) a *pig* as an insult started in the 1500s and that term for a police officer dates to 1811. A *flying pig* being something impossible dates back to 1610.

Rats

Rats leaving a sinking ship is a phrase used now to talk about staff leaving a failing enterprise or any movement of disloyal people. The original phrase described actual *rats* and dates back to the 1500s. Sailors believed if *rats* jumped off a ship, it was an ill omen. It's mentioned in "The Tempest" (1610) by William Shakespeare.

Rat is one of those common words whose origins are obscure and yet shared among many different languages. It first entered Old English as *raet* and there are similar words in Romanic, Celtic, and Germanic languages. The association of *rats* with abandoning sinking ships and always looking after themselves before others is the origin of the use of their name to tag informants and the phrase *to smell a rat*.

As a result of their fore-knowledge of evil events, *rats* were regarded by sailors as lucky creatures.

Selkie

A *selkie*, or *silkie*, is a legendary sea creature who wears the appearance of a seal, but inside is a beautiful woman. A man who is lucky enough to find such a creature by the shore should take and hide the discarded skin of the *selkie* before marrying her. She will be a loyal wife and raise beautiful human children but if she ever finds the skin, she will regain her true nature and return to the sea.

Such *seal-wife* tales were widespread in Ireland and Scotland in particular, although the details changed with location. The *seal-wife* might enjoy eating her fish raw, or a certain family might be rumoured to be descended from seals.

Whale

Whales, as the largest creatures in the sea, are not lacking in monstrous stories inspired by their sheer size.

There are tales of *whale islands*, Jonah being swallowed by a *whale* in the Bible, the leviathan (see the Old Sea Dog Tales chapter), and even stories of witches turning into *whales* to herd the fish into the nets of the boats belonging to their families.

Whale entered Old English as *hwael* (*whale* or walrus) from Saxon *hwal*, Norse *hvalr*, Swedish *val*, and German *wal*.

To have *a whale of a time* is from student slang in 1900 where *whale* is used to indicate large or excellent. *To whale*, meaning to beat, may relate to the stripes left upon a body afterwards reminding people of the stripes on a *whale*.

8. Maritime Manoeuvres

If you want to pass as a salty sea dog rather than a landlubber, you'll need to understand the following terms. The things we do on a ship, or indeed to a ship, have in many cases passed onto land and into the dictionary. Here's a selection of maritime manoeuvres for you and your crew.

Bail

Bail has two core meanings in English, one shore-based and one ship-based. The noun *bail* - gaining temporary release for a prisoner - dates back to the 1300s. The verb *bail* is more recent (1610s) and describes scooping out water using a small bucket. This is a vital task if your ship is leaking or water has come in over the side. This, combined with the idea of the prison release, gives us the concept of a financial *bail-out* for a broken bank or bankrupt economy.

A *baile* was a small wooden bucket in English from the mid 1400s, probably from Old French *baille* (a pail) and ultimately from Medieval Latin *baiula aquae* (a porter of water). This type of *bailing* on ships gave us the idea of *bailing out* for pilots (from 1930s) for any sort of sudden exit.

More recently *bail* is the term used by surfers who jump off their boards to avoid a wipe-out.

Careen
{with thanks to ZZNewell on Critique Circle}

Careen means to sway from side perilously - a drunken cyclist might *careen* comically through a busy fruit market, for example. But its primary meaning is in relation to boats. To *careen* a boat means to tip it over to show its hull, generally in order to repair it or scrape it clear of barnacles and sea detritus.

Garbage attached to the hull will influence the fluid dynamics. However while your ship is out of the water you're vulnerable to attack and unable to earn through trade or piracy, so deciding to *careen* was a tricky balancing act, something like *careening* itself.

Careen comes from the Latin *carina* (keel of a ship). Sometimes the meanings of *careen* and *career* are confused. *Careen* is to lurch from side to side, while *career* is to rush in.

Cruising

Cruising, in the sense of sailing to and fro, entered English in the 1650s from the Dutch verb *kruisen* (to sail, to cross) and ultimately from Latin *crux* (cross) which also gives us *crucifix*.

It was 1906 before the word became a noun describing a sea voyage taken by tourists.

The later meaning of *cruising* in a car, or *cruise* control, or indeed the social activity of *cruising*, came about by comparison with sailing *cruises*.

Float

To *float* is to rest on the surface of the water and it's an old English word with German roots. The Old English version *flotian* is related to Old Norse *flota*, Middle Dutch *vloten* and Old High German *flozzan* or *flössen* – all of whom actually come back to the idea of flowing.

Floating as a form of drifting was the original meaning but by 1600 there was a more active sense of setting something *afloat* and it wasn't long until it gained financial overtones with *floating a company* (1700s) and airborne *floating* (1600s).

It wasn't until the 1900s that we got a drink called a *float* with the addition of ice cream to a soda, where the ice cream *floats* at the top of the tall glass.

Launch

Launch has been a verb in English since the 1300s and means to rush or leap. It came from the Old French word *lancher* and ultimately from Late Latin *lanceare* – to wield a light lance.

It's difficult to imagine the idea of a light spear flying through the air inspiring the term for the ungainly pushing required to *launch* a boat for her maiden voyage, but that's what is claimed happened by the mid 1400s.

Then by the 1690s there's a small boat called a *launch* carried on warships, probably from a combination of the Portuguese *lancha* (barge, *launch*) and *lancher* (quick, agile) in Malay. It took until 1935 for the term *launch* to be applied to missile liftoffs and the term has stuck, perhaps with more justification as a space rocket looks more like a spear, than a huge aircraft carrier ever will.

Ship *launches* are rich in seafaring superstitions. The use of a liquid on the hull of a ship during its naming ceremony may even link back to the days of blood sacrifice. The use of a champagne bottle is most common now but in the 1700s the health of the ship was drunk from a silver cup which was then thrown into the sea. Was it an extravagant gesture or an offering to the sea gods?

Bungling the breaking of the bottle often gives the ship a bad reputation thereafter.

Now it's not only vehicles and vessels which are *launched* with bottles of wine – it has been known to apply to *company launches* and *book launches* too, although breaking open the bottle is easier with a corkscrew than with the nautical smashing method.

Leeway

Leeway is a compound word in English since the 1660s to describe the sideways drifting of a ship in her course caused by wind. Clearly this was a problem to the ship's navigator but it wasn't until the 1800s that the term gained a shoreside meaning.

From 1827 it was used to describe any loss of progress and from 1835 it was used to mean extra space. For example "the woman's dress was so huge that customers stepped aside to give her *leeway*". The meaning of extra space doesn't relate to *leeway's* nautical use.

Overhaul

Most often used in the sense of *overhauling* an engine or other technical setup now. The idea of *overhauling* originated on sailing ships.

Overhaul entered English in the 1600s as a compound of *over* and *haul* and the meaning was to pull rigging apart so it could be examined. Fixing and replacing frayed ropes on a sailing ship was a frequent task.

To loosen the rigging for inspection required the crew to *haul* in the opposite direction to when they'd hoisted it in the first place.

The idea of *overhaul* meaning to *overtake* (used more commonly in American English than in British English) only arose in the late 1700s and was a replacement for the term *overhale*.

Salvage

Salvage entered English in the 1640s to describe a payment made for saving a ship from wreck or capture and the word came from Old French *salver* (to save). Using *salvage* to describe the recycling of waste didn't arise until 1918, from World War One.

The right to *salvage* ships was a valuable one and has an unusual horse-riding legend associated with it. The Trevelyan family (and some others) have a horse's head rising from the waves on their heraldry. This is explained as symbolising their ancient right to claim *salvage* from a wreck if one of their family could ride into the waves and touch the wreck with the tip of a lance.

In the 1100s there was a Breton legend, probably explaining coastal erosion which is common on the coast of Brittany, of land swallowed suddenly by the sea because a king's daughter opened sluices and the sea rushed in. Only the king survived by galloping so fast on his horse ahead of the waves. The English adopted the tale in the 1500s and applied it to the Trevelyan coat of arms.

Shanty
{with thanks to Paul Powell on CritiqueCircle}

A *shanty* is a sea song, originally spelled *chanty*. The *shanties* were work songs from the 1800s, giving tall ship sail crews the rhythm and team spirit needed to do heavy tasks.

Shanty, is from Latin *cantare* (to sing) via French *chanter* (to sing). It is unrelated to the concept of *shanty shack* and *shantytowns*. Sailors also sang fo'c's'le songs about their experiences ashore - typically cautionary tales about being seduced and robbed.

Certain *shanties* are associated with specific tasks. The *chanty man* often led the singing and would adapt the lyrics depending on the nationality of the crew. In long *shanties* the later verses became increasingly ribald.

One specific task that had its own song was the Dead Horse Ceremony. After one month at sea the sailors had worked off their advance of one month's wages (usually spent ashore before departure) and celebrated getting paid again by singing the Dead Horse Song and dragging a canvas straw-stuffed effigy of a horse about the decks, hoisting it aloft, and throwing it overboard. The chorus of the song went "They say my horse is dead and gone. Oh poor old man!"

As steam ships replaced sailing ships, *shanties* reduced in popularity but many folk groups, male voice choirs, and specialist *shanty* groups keep them alive.

Whelmed

Whelmed isn't a commonly-used verb although it is regularly found in the more expansive form of *overwhelmed* (overcome with emotions or experiences) and *underwhelmed* (lacking in inspiration and energy), but you <u>will</u> find it in the classic American novel "Moby Dick".

In fact the verb *whelmed* has three, related, meanings -

1. to turn a dish or vessel upside down to cover something. To engulf something, possibly with disastrous results.

2. to be overcome in thoughts or emotions (sounds awfully like *overwhelmed*)

3. to go over something and hence bury or submerge it

This means *overwhelmed* is completely over the top when you consider meaning number two.

Whelm entered English in the late 1200s via Middle English *whelme* which was a combination of a dialect word *whelve* (from Old English *gehwelfan* – to bend over) and *helm* (Old English – to cover) – the idea being a vessel being turned over or covered in something.

Whelming can be applied to boats, submarines, perfumes, and even cooking dishes. The next time you flip a cake from a tin using a plate, you'll be *whelming*.

9. Eponymous Words from the Sea

Eponyms are the words in the dictionary which were given to English from people's names. For example, the humble sandwich, lunch of millions, was named after the Earl of Sandwich who was rather fond of them when he was working late or gambling late (there's some dispute about his work ethic).

Nautical words contain a few eponyms too and they're gathered here, along with toponyms (words named after places rather than people – *aran sweaters*, *bermuda shorts* for example). The sea had a big influence on shore-based clothes and it's not all sou'westers.

If you enjoy this selection of eponyms, check out my earlier book about eponyms, "How To Get Your Name In The Dictionary", widely available in paperback and ebook formats.

Aphrodisiac

An *aphrodisiac* is a food or drink deemed to stimulate sexual desire. They are named for *Aphrodite*, the Greek goddess of love and beauty. According to Homer she was born from the sea foam as daughter of Dione and Zeus.

Zeus, fearing the gods would fight over her amazing beauty married her off quickly to Hephaestus, the smith god. He showered her with jewellery and crafted a magical girdle of finely wrought gold for her. Unfortunately it increased her appeal and her infidelity was legendary.

Her festival, *Aphrodisiac*, was celebrated around Greece. The Greeks believed intercourse with her priestesses was the best way to worship *Aphrodite*. *April,* the month when Spring romance in nature gets underway in Europe, is named for her.

Aran Sweater

Aran sweaters, sometimes called fisherman sweaters (or *aran jumpers* in Ireland), are wool sweaters knitted originally on the *Aran islands* off the Atlantic coast of Ireland. They are known for their complex raised patterns and have been associated with some wonderful legends.

Nowadays the sweaters, sold by the truckload to tourists, are usually machine-knitted in a soft pale cream shade but originally they were hand-crafted in darker colours for the fishermen of the islands and the wool would have been unrefined to make it rain resistant.

The sweaters were made from the fleece of the islander's own sheep and each could take 50 hours to create. Up to 24 stitch patterns were used with each woman knitting her own version of the garment. White or cream sweaters were made in smaller sizes for youngsters making their Holy Communion.

Early documentaries about island life in the 1930s (long before running water and electricity came to the islands) popularised the island's crafts. With help from the Craft Council of Ireland and early members of the Irish Countrywomen's Association (an organisation similar to the Women's Institute in Britain) islanders began crafting and exporting sweaters in the lighter colour for overseas shoppers.

Each stitch has a meaning associated with life on the island. Cable represents the ropes on the boats, diamond represents hopes for future wealth, honeycomb represents hard work like the bees of the island, and the zig zag stitch represents the cliffs.

Legend has it that each family's sweater pattern was unique and acted as a method of identifying drowned fishermen. This legend is shared with similar sweaters from the Channel Islands, but in the case of *Aran* it is unlikely. The islanders formed a small community and missing fishermen would have been known by all.

Just as today, expert knitters varied patterns for the sheer joy of it. *Aran weight yarn* (worsted weight in North America) is named for the islands too and is used in creating the sweaters.

Bermuda Shorts

The story of these formal dress shorts begins with a very British cup of tea.

In World War I the British navy established their North Atlantic headquarters on the island of *Bermuda*. Local man Nathanial Coxon owned a tea-shop in *Bermuda* and it quickly saw a boom in custom from naval officers. The steam from the tea pots made it a hot spot and his staff complained their uniform of a smart navy blazer teamed with khaki trousers was stifling. Coxon, a thrifty man, shortened all the trousers to just above the knee.

When Rear Admiral Mason Berridge took his tea at Coxon's he admired the look, dubbed them *Bermuda Shorts*, and adopted them for his officers. He always gave credit to Coxon, who was later awarded an OBE (Order of the British Empire).

The Royal Navy uniform still includes the shorts.

The idea of wearing knee-high socks with the shorts came about in World War II. Two bank managers in *Bermuda* ordered the shorts for their employees, due to fabric shortages, and paired them with long socks. The look was a fashion smash, local shops copied it and it's now the island's national dress. Businessmen wear the short and sock combo all year round. During the Olympic opening ceremony the Bermudian team usually sport red *Bermuda shorts* as red is the main colour in their flag.

Not everyone was happy about so much leg being on show. Once policemen were armed with a tape measure and a ticket book and sent out to ensure that the menfolk weren't showing more than six inches of leg.

Bikini

On the 5th of July 1946 French designer Louis Réard (1897-1984) unveiled a daring two-piece swimsuit in Paris. He named it the *bikini* after the *Bikini Atoll* in the Pacific Ocean which had hosted an U.S. atomic test earlier that week.

Réard was a gifted marketeer, happy to hop on the coat-tails of the headline-grabbing tests. He also claimed you couldn't call a two-piece a real *bikini* unless it could pass through a wedding ring.

In his hunt for a model willing to bare nearly all in front of the world's press, he chose Micheline Bernardini - a Parisian showgirl/exotic dancer. He used newspaper style print on the fabric as a reference to the headlines he knew the garment would produce and unsurprisingly the *bikini* was a huge hit. Bernardini received 50,000 fan letters.

The two-piece wasn't new. Greek and Roman women were depicted wearing them in art from antiquity. Modern Europeans had worn them as halter tops with shorts during the 1930s but beach life was essentially impossible in Europe during World War II thanks to coastline fortifications and land mines. The 1946 *bikini* marked a post-war return to the shoreline.

Young women wearing the new fashion created a scandal along the beaches of Europe. Spain and Italy outlawed them but by the 1950s, perhaps thanks to iconic photographs of Brigit Bardot at the 1953 Cannes Film Festival, the *bikini* had eroded resistance.

The *bikini* won over America in the early 1960s with the rise of a younger, liberated generation who bopped along to the Beach Boys and Brian Hyland's "Itsy, Bitsy, Teenie, Weenie, Yellow Polka Dot *Bikini*".

Blazer

In the early days of the Royal Navy captains were allowed to issue whatever clothes they deemed fit to their crew out of their own pockets. As a result most crews didn't wear uniforms but some richer captains issued uniforms for ceremonial events.

The crew of *HMS Harlequin* wore harlequin outfits. The crew of *HMS Caledonia* wore tartan. The unfortunate crew of *HMS Tulip* had green suits with flowers in their caps. In 1837, the *HMS Blazer* adopted a navy jacket teamed with blue and white striped jerseys for a royal visit by Queen Victoria. Over time the navy blue look became standard within the navy.

Bristol Fashion / Ship-shape

The phrase *"ship-shape and Bristol Fashion"*, from the 1800s, has surprising links to the British slave trade.

Bristol was a great port on the "triangular trade". Merchants exported manufactured goods to Africa where the ships then collected slaves to sell in the Caribbean plantations, where they picked up cargos of raw materials like sugar, cotton, chocolate, and tobacco bound for Europe. On each leg of the triangular journey the ship-owners made a profit. Slavery wasn't abolished in the British Empire until 1833.

The slave ships not only stank but also carried disease, so the citizens of the prosperous merchant town of *Bristol* wouldn't allow them to dock until they were cleaned and made tidy. Before they entered the harbour the ships were inspected to ensure they were *ship-shape and Bristol fashion*.

Additionally, *Bristol* port had the second highest tidal range in the world at the time – 13 metres (43 feet) – so ships moored in the area would be aground at low tide and tilt to one side. If everything wasn't tied down and stowed away properly it would be chaotic.

Davy Jones' Locker

Davy Jones' locker is at the bottom of the sea and is mariners' slang for the final resting place of drowned sailors.

It is unlikely that there was a real *Davy Jones*, despite the character in "The Pirates of the Caribbean" movies. Various candidates exist, however.

Jones may be a corruption of the biblical figure, Jonah, who was swallowed by a whale. Jonah was seen as a bad luck figure by superstitious seafarers because his tale involved a boat in peril.

The patron saint of sailors is St. David (also the patron saint of Wales, he's a busy chap) and David is often shortened to *Davy*, so that might give us the first name. *Jones* is also a popular Welsh surname. Dying is a way of joining the saints so the locker could be heaven in this case.

"Brewer's Dictionary of Phrase and Fable" claims the term comes from a combination of things – the *locker* being the safe place for a sailor to store something (their soul), *Jones* from the story of Jonah (who was sent overboard) and *Davy* from duffy (a word for a ghost or evil spirit in the West Indies).

An alternative tale springs from a 1594 ballad, "Jones' Ale is Newe", which tells of a publican *Davy Jones*. He gathered drunken sailors in his bar and stored them safely in the ale lockers at the back of the inn, then sold them to the press gang. The drunks woke aboard ship and served out their voyage while *Jones* pocketed their sign-on fees.

In J.M. Barrie's novel "Peter and Wendy", Captain Hook sings;

> *"Yo ho, yo ho, the frisky plank.*
> *You walks along it so.*
> *Till it goes down and you goes*
> *Down to Davy Jones below!"*

There is a long-standing tradition of celebrating crossing the equator by paying homage to *Davy Jones*.

Those who have crossed it before play the part of Neptune and Neptune's sons or shellbacks. This is observed in many national navies. Those who are new to the crossing are called pollywogs. The ceremony can get rough and has been prohibited in a few cases.

Derrick

A *derrick* is a single spar lifting-hoist commonly used to move cargo from ship to quayside or vice versa, and until the advent of helicopters used to hoist lighthouse keepers from rowboats onto lighthouse rock stations. The *derrick* takes its name from *Thomas Derrick*, an Elizabethan executioner.

Thomas Derrick was found guilty of outraging women during the 1596 Sack of Cadiz in Spain. He was sentenced to be flogged around the fleet.

A sailor sentenced to this punishment was rowed between all the ships in the fleet so sailors could witness his flogging. The sentence could take months or even years to complete. After each flogging was completed his back would be washed with sea water in a vain attempt to arrest infections. This gave rise to the expression *rubbing salt into a wound*.

To avoid his fate *Derrick* agreed to inflict the same punishment on his fellow convicts and later became executioner at Tyburn in London. He was pardoned by Robert Devereux, the 2nd Earl of Essex whom he later executed with an axe in 1601 for treason.

Derrick devised a beam with a lift and pulleys for his role as hangman rather than the traditional rope over a beam method.

He executed 3,000 people during his career.

Fudging (the Books)

This expression comes from *Captain Fudge* of *The Black Eagle*.

Lying Fudge, as he was known, was commissioned in August 1665 to transport 55 Quakers from Britain to the colonies as punishment for offences against the Conventicle Act which outlawed religious meetings other than those of the Church of England.

His departure was delayed. By October a third of the prisoners had died of plague, along with some crew.

When he was arrested for debt, the remaining crew mutinied. In February 1666 the ship finally set sail for the West Indies but she was seized by a Dutch privateer and the Quakers were freed.

He spun such a false tale of this adventure in his ship's logbook that his name entered the language as a word for a great lie, especially as told by a sailor.

Gibraltar

Gibraltar's name comes from *Gebel Tarik*, meaning Tarik's mountain. Tarik was a Moorish chief who conquered the place in 711 and built a castle on the rock.

The Moors held it until 1309 when the Spanish took it for a while, then the Moors again. The Spanish held it (1462-1704) until it was seized by Sir George Rooke for Britain. By 1783 Spain decided to forego her claim to the rock in favour of her claims on Florida and Minorca (Spain sold Florida to the U.S.A. in 1809).

In total there were 13 naval sieges of *Gibraltar* throughout history, including one during the Second World War. As a result you may raise a glass to the *Siege of Gibraltar* on any date in the calendar year – the perfect excuse for a drink.

Gimlette

A *gimlette* is a drink of gin and lime juice.

The naval Surgeon Admiral Sir Thomas *Gimlette* (1857-1943) concocted this beverage to convince sailors to drink fruit juice and hence avoid scurvy.

It's possible Sir Thomas didn't make this order effective in the navy as it wasn't mentioned in his obituary, but that never stood in the way of a good story. The image of the respected doctor ordering up cocktails as medicine is hard to resist.

Grog & Groggy

Grog is any diluted spirits, usually rum, given to sailors. This nautical tipple was named for *Old Grog*, the nickname of British admiral Sir Edward Vernon (1684-1757). He issued *grog* rations to the sailors on his ship in 1740 to end drunken brawling on board thanks to the straight rum which was normally issued to the crew. Dilution reduced the drunkenness, but didn't remove alcohol entirely from the ship.

The dilution proportions varied and gained compass-related names. "Due North" was pure rum while "Due West" was water only.

Grog rations failed to eradicate discipline issues and the quantities were tweaked for many years, once even by the wonderfully-named *Admiralty's Grog Committee*.

Grog also gives us the word *groggy* which was originally used to describe a hangover from excess consumption of *grog*.

Old Grog, who became a vice admiral at the young age of 24, gained his nickname by wearing a cloak made of *grogram* during bad weather. *Grogram* was a coarse fabric made of wool and mohair or silk.

Grog blossom was seafaring slang for the redness on the face of someone who drinks *grog* to excess.

The *grog* ration was finally eradicated in the Royal Navy in 1970 after the British parliament held the Great Rum Debate.

By Hook or By Crook

This phrase means to use whatever means necessary to achieve an objective.

There are several competing stories for its origins.

In medieval England a feudal custom allowed peasants to harvest wood from royal forests but only what they could pull down with a shepherd's *crook* or cut with a reaper's *billhook*. This was an important concession in a time when the crown owned huge forests. Hunting on the king's estates would land you on the gallows but at least they could warm their families. The combination of *hook* and *crook* allegedly gave us the phrase although it's hard to see that using a simple hand tool is the same as using whatever means are necessary.

The alternative Irish legend says when Oliver Cromwell (1599-1658) was laying siege to Waterford city in 1649-1650 he claimed it would fall to his forces "*by hook or by crook*". The town could be entered by landing an army at either *Hook* Head with its famous ancient lighthouse or via *Crook* village on the opposite side of the channel. The problem with this story is that the phrase is used in English documents in the 1300s, predating Cromwell's campaign to subdue Ireland.

A more likely tale, again Irish, relates to an earlier English visitor – King Richard III (1452-1485).

The voyage to Ireland from England could be perilous, depending on weather, and many ships sank. The two most extreme points on the southern Irish coast where King Richard could harbour safely were *Hook* Head in County Wexford or *Crookhaven* in County Cork, further west. If they overshot the inlets between these two points they would be swept around to the western coast of Ireland which was known to be treacherous and indeed dealt punishing blows to the Spanish Armada in the late 1500s because of their lack of charts and the wild weather. Therefore the Normans vowed to land *by Hook or by Crook*.

My own theory is that all three are correct. The feudal firewood custom would have been known to King Richard III and his nobles, thus leading to their vow to steer for *Hook or Crook*(haven). Such navigation advice was probably still in use by Cromwell's time so it's not surprising that he'd adopt the same approach to conquering the south coast. Cromwell and his army had a devastating effect on Ireland so it's understandable that his use of the phrase is the one that stuck in the collective memory.

Hunky Dory

Hunky dory is an expression meaning everything is fine. Its spelling has varied widely over time with *hunkey dorey* being one of the earliest in print, in an 1862 American song. By 1866 it was *hunkee doree* or *hunky-dore*.

That variation in spelling suggests it was verbal slang. *Hunkey* was also used around that time for something being fit, healthy, and ready for action.

There's strong evidence to suggest that *hunky dory* originated in Japan rather than America and then travelled with mariners to American shores.

Commodore Matthew Perry (1794-1858) opened up trade to Japan in the 1850s by use of gunboat diplomacy and smart treaties. He is considered the father of the steam navy and fought hard to establish proper training academies for the U.S. Navy.

By the 1860s (when *hunky dory* arrived in American English) there were frequent voyages between the two countries. Japanese for "main street" is *honcho-dori*.

American sailors would have known the word *hunky* and may have either substituted it or misheard *honcho*. There were *honcho-dori* or *honki-dori* streets in both Tokyo and Yokohama which had a large number of friendly young ladies residing there to provide solace to long-distance sailors.

India Pale Ale

With the rise of the hipster came the rise of craft beers. Many of them had *IPA* on the packaging.

IPA stands for *India pale ale*, a hoppy beer style dispatched to the British Empire in the east when London still ruled India. It was too hot to brew beer over there so colonial suppliers needed a beer that could survive the six month sea voyage.

A London brewer called George Hodgson sold beers to the East India Company whose headquarters lay a few miles downriver of his brewery.

The East India Company and the army became frustrated with Hodgson's quality so he tried unfermented beer with yeast added on arrival. He tried shipping beer concentrate for dilution on arrival. His final effort was October Ale, a strong heavily hopped beer, which he created to be aged like wine. He intended it to replace wine which was scarce thanks to the long Napoleonic wars with France.

In 1822 it survived the trip and actually improved on the way. *IPAs* gradually became paler and lighter after that point to eventually give us modern-style *IPAs*.

Over time the *IPAs* fell out of favour in Britain but they were revived by craft brewers in America in the 1970s.

Joe

Joe is U.S. slang for a cup of coffee.

Joe is named for Josephus Daniels (1862-1948). Josephus was Woodrow Wilson's Secretary of the Navy and abolished the officers' wine mess aboard naval ships in 1914, thus leaving coffee as the strongest drink on board.

Neptune

Originally believed to be a star, John Couch Adams and Urban Le Verrier calculated planet Neptune's location.

Johann Galle who discovered the planet in 1846 thanks to their calculations wanted to name it Verrier in their honour but other astronomers objected.

Other names were suggested; such as Janus and Oceanus. By the end of the year *Neptune*, the Roman god of the seas, was settled upon which is appropriate as the planet is a bright sea blue.

Neptune's astronomical symbol is a stylised version of *Neptune's* trident.

Plimsolls and the Plimsoll Line

The *plimsoll line* is painted around a ship's hull to indicate the safe loading level at a glance. If the mark is underwater, the ship is overloaded. It is named in honour of *Samuel Plimsoll* (1824-1898), a shipping reformer.

Plimsoll left school early, started as a brewery clerk, and worked his way up to manager. He was then a coal dealer but went bankrupt and lived in very reduced circumstances which sparked his sympathy for the poor when his fortunes recovered.

In 1868 he was elected MP for the land-locked constituency of Derby. He called the routinely overloaded ships of his day "coffin ships". They were often heavily insured and the unscrupulous owners risked the lives of their crew knowing they wouldn't lose money if they sank. He campaigned for safety improvements in maritime traffic despite the many ship-owning members of parliament.

In 1872 a compromise bill was introduced to deal with the issue and *Plimsoll* accepted it, reluctantly. When Disraeli announced the bill was to be dropped *Plimsoll* called his parliamentary colleagues villains and shook his fist in the Speaker's face, outraged that pressure from ship-owners had stifled it.

Eventually he apologised for his behaviour but popular opinion admired his honesty and a year later the government was forced to make rigorous inspections of ships compulsory. *The Plimsoll Line*, was adopted in the same year. This simple line of paint has saved thousands of lives at sea.

In the 1920s *plimsolls*, rubber-soled canvas shoes, came to bear his name because the line on the rubber sole reminded wearers of the *plimsoll line*.

Shanghaied or Shanghai Press

Shanghaiing is the practice of kidnapping people to serve as crew on sailing ships. *Pressing* or *press ganging* is the related term for kidnapping them to serve in the British Royal Navy. This practice also gave us the expression *pressed into service*.

Shanghaiing wasn't that common in *Shanghai*, it was the destination port rather than the source. Sailors and bystanders would be *shanghaied* from London, Bristol, Hull, San Francisco, Portland, New York, Boston etc.

The practice arose due to a chronic lack of experienced sailors in the mid 1800s. This was due, in part, to crews absconding en masse to try their hand at prospecting in the Californian Gold Rush.

Once a sailor signed on for a voyage it was against the law for him to leave before it was over. Boarding masters were in charge of sourcing enough sailors for the crew and they got paid per person. They had a big incentive to get someone on board, even if they had to get them drunk first or forge their signature on the crew list.

The *shanghai press* wasn't finally outlawed until 1915 when the end of the Age of Sail meant the demand for crew lessened.

In Chinese the word *Shanghai* means "upon the sea".

Sweet Fanny Adams

This expression, meaning "nothing at all", dates to 1867 when an eight year old English girl called *Fanny Adams* (1859-1867) was found dismembered and mutilated. Her murderer, Frederick Baker, left pieces of her body in a field in Alton, Hampshire where her grave can be seen to this day. Baker, who was a solicitor's clerk, was convicted and hanged on Christmas Eve 1867.

At that time Royal Navy sailors were issued with canned mutton as a staple part of their diet. It was of poor quality and became known as *sweet fanny adams* because it was chopped up. Over time this mutated to mean anything worthless or even "nothing at all".

The tins the mutton came in were often re-used as mess tins or cooking pots and these are still called *fannys*.

10. I Do Like to Be Beside the Seaside

There's something special about the shoreline, the line where the sea means the land. The line itself constantly changes with the tides and erosion but it's a threshold, a place of magic and peace. If you've ever wandered along the beach, eyes downcast for the glint of sea-glass and ears filled with the roar of surf or the gentle shush of water trickling onto shells, then you know this.

All the items in this chapter can be found on the shoreline and are related to the sea. Ships have to dock somewhere and landlubbers do like to be beside the seaside.

Bollard

A *bollard*, which entered English in the late 1800s, was originally a strong upright post to which you might tie your vessel. It's a compound word of *bole* (the truck of a tree) and *–ard*.

–Ard is a suffix used to intensify the first part of the word. It's found in *dullard, drunkard, coward, dastard, dotard, laggard, bastard*, and in the lesser known *blaffard* – one who stammers.

Since 1948 a *bollard* is more commonly seen as a device for controlling car traffic.

Buoy

A *buoy* is a floating warning of a channel or an underwater hazard. *Buoy* came into English in the 1200s as *boie*, probably from Old French *buie* or Middle Dutch *boeye*. These either came from *baukna*, a Proto-Germanic word for beacon or signal, or from Old French *boie* (chain) because the float is chained in place.

The pronunciation of *buoy* varies from "boy" to "boo-E" depending on your birthplace. If you lean towards the "boo-E" version I'd love to know how you pronounce *bouyancy*.

The adjective *buoyant* refers to something floating but since the 1700s can also refer to a person on land who is upbeat in mood and attitude.

Causeway

A *causeway* is a raised path or road above the level of the natural ground around it. They're associated with islands surrounded by sea water or marshes which are accessible on foot via such a path at low tide.

Causeway has been used in English since the 1570s but the concept is older, originating with Latin *calx* (heel) and *calciare* (to stamp with heels) – the idea being a path was made through marsh land by trampling down the ground to be firmer. This led to *via calciata* (a paved way) from *calx'* second meaning (limestone).

Thereafter the *via calciata* travelled through French as *cauce* and *cauceweye* (raised road) to reach *causeway* in English.

The drama of the tide rushing over a *causeway* attracted many storytellers. The most miraculous tale is of Saint Cuthbert's *causeway*.

Cuthbert was bishop of the holy island of Lindisfarne in Northumberland and after his death he was buried there. When Vikings attacked in the 9th century the monks removed his body for safekeeping to Durham but in 1069 he had to be moved again, to avoid William the Conqueror. The monks intended returning him to Lindisfarne but when they reached the *causeway* to the island the tide was in full flood.

The monks bewailed the delay but the waves parted and they crossed dry-footed with their saint, the waves closing behind them and preventing pursuit.

Dock

Long before you *docked* your phone for charging or to play music, and before an accused stood confined before a judge, boats were *docking* to load cargo or for repair.

A *dock* is a ship's birth or any structure upon which a ship may be held. For example a ship needs a *dry dock* for hull repairs or painting.

The word *dock* has humble origins with the Scandinavian word for low ground. It's likely the first *dock* was a simple furrow in the shoreline. From there it travelled to Middle Dutch and Middle Low German as *docke* and *dokke* and finally in the late 1400s to English.

Estuary & Fjord

Estuary, the tidal area at the mouth of a river, entered English in the 1530s from the Latin word *aestuarium* (a tidal marsh). *Aestuarium* derives from *aestus* (burning) perhaps because the water bubbled as if boiling.

Several cities and other words come from *estuary*.

A *firth*, describing an *estuary* or arm of the sea in Scotland came unsurprisingly from Scottish to English in the early 1400s, probably from the Old Norse word *fjordr* for *fjord*.

Fjord itself entered English in the 1600s from the Norwegian word *fjord* and its own roots are in Proto-Germanic *ferthuz* – a place for crossing over, a *ford*.

Oslo, the capital of Norway, is named for an Old Norse word, *os*, for a tidal *estuary* or river mouth because of Oslo's position.

Tokyo was named in 1868, but its original name was *Edo*, meaning *estuary*.

Rio de Janeiro translates directly as January River. It was thus named by Amerigo Verspucci (see America in the Maps & Navigation chapter) on the first of January 1502 because he thought, incorrectly, that the bay it sits upon was the *estuary* of a river.

Flotsam & Jetsam

Both *flotsam* and *jetsam* are maritime legal terms indicating different types of shipwreck.

Flotsam is floating wreckage of a ship or its cargo e.g. a mast ripped off a yacht in a storm. It comes from Old

English and German words for floating and its first known usage is 1607.

Jetsam is part of a ship, its equipment, or cargo which is cast overboard (*jettisoned*) deliberately in time of distress. It may then sink or wash ashore e.g. throwing an empty crate or water barrel overboard to lighten the load in a storm. It sounds like sea littering to me. *Jetsam* is a variation of *jettison* and was first used c. 1591.

There's also *lagan or ligan* (cargo on the seabed which can be reclaimed) and *derelict* (cargo on the seabed which nobody has a hope of reclaiming).

Gabion

Gabion, from the old Italian word for a large cage, is a wire cage filled with stones used in construction projects and sea defences against erosion.

Groin (or groyne)

A *groin* is a long narrow structure in coastal engineering built out into the water to prevent beach erosion by trapping sand. It stabilises the beach on the updrift side but may cause issues in the other direction. As a result they are often built in groups known as *groin fields*.

Groin joined the English language in the 1500s as a dialect word meaning "snout". That in turn came from Old French *groign* and Latin words *grunium* "pig's snout" and *grunnire* a verb meaning "to grunt". The next time I spy a line of timber posts running out to sea to disrupt erosion I will think of the land as snuffling its way out into the pig trough of waves.

Gulf

A *gulf* on land is a type of ravine, whereas at sea it is an area of ocean surrounded by land on three sides, a deep inlet with a narrow mouth. A famous example is the *Gulf* of Mexico and it gives us the equally famous ocean current the *Gulf Stream*.

The idea of a *gulf* between people or opinions comes from the marine version.

Gulf entered English to describe something smaller than a sea but larger than a bay around 1400 and it starts with the Greeks. Greek has the word *kolpos* to describe a gulf of the sea but it originally related to the trough between waves, the folds of a garment, or bosom – the general idea being curves.

Kolpos migrated into Latin as *colfos* and from there to Italian as *golfo*. French took it next as *golf* (a *gulf* or whirlpool, nothing to do with a popular outdoor sport) and finally it landed as *gulf* in English.

Harbour or Harbor

A *harbour* is usually a safe dwelling place for boats and that's where it entered Middle English in the early 1100s as *herberwe*. It has even older roots in *here-beorg* (Saxon*)*, *here-berg* (Anglian), and *herbergi* (Old Norse, lodgings).

The idea of ships having a safe recess in the coastline eventually gave rise to the concept of safe *harbour* for people ashore too. The use of *harbour* as a verb meaning to give shelter came about in the 1300s and later gained a more figurative meaning where somebody *harbours* thoughts about something.

Haven

A *haven* is a place of refuge. In nautical terms it's an inlet or small harbour providing shelter for boats. In news reports it appears you can only have the word *haven* if it's preceded by safe.

Haven is one the Vikings gave us. Old Norse has *höfn* (*haven* or harbour) and that passed into Old English as *haefen*.

The city of Copenhagen's name is compounded of *copen* (meaning cheap) and *havn* (haven), something the Copenhagen tourist board keeps pretty quiet.

Jetty

A *jetty* is a long narrow structure projecting from the shore into the water. They can be used to tie up smaller boats, to protect the coastline from currents and tides, or to connect the land to areas of deeper water for larger ships to moor. The stairs used to access a jet plane are also called a *jetty*.

Jetty has Roman and French word roots. The Latin verb *iacere* means to throw. This moved into French as the verb *jeter* with the same meaning. Old French developed the related word *jetee* or *getee* to describe a *jetty*, pier or projecting part of a building from the idea of a structure being thrown out beyond its surroundings. In the early 1400s *jetee* became *jetty* in English.

There is a spiral *jetty* on the Great Salt Lake in Utah. Created by artist Robert Smithson in 1970 it twists in a circular spiral and has become a tourist attraction.

Lagoon

Lagoon, like quarantine (see the Salmagundi chapter), is one of the words the watery city of Venice has given to English. *Lagoons* entered the language in the 1670s to describe an area of marsh or shallow, brackish water between a sea but separated from it by dunes. Originally spelled as *laguna* or *lagune*, it came from Italian *laguna* (pond or lake) and ultimately from Latin *lacuna* (pond). It took until 1769 and Captain Cook to discover that the *lagoons* in the South Seas were less brackish and more sparkling.

Mooring

To *moor* a vessel is to fasten it in place with the use of ropes, cables, or anchors. The word entered English in the 1400s as the Old English word *maerels* and may have been a borrowing from Middle Low German *moren* or Middle Dutch *maren*.

Mooring is unrelated to the term *Moor* to describe somebody from North Africa or the Barbary coast. Although it is wonderful to discover that *morris* dancing (a popular U.K. folk dance) was originally called *Moorish* dancing.

Pier

A *pier* wasn't always a manmade structure jutting out from land for mooring ships. The earliest use of *pier*, in the mid 1100s, related to bridges. The *pier* was the support for a span of bridge, the part that went into the water. It came from Medieval Latin *pera*, possibly from Old North French *pire* (breakwater), and ultimately from Latin *petra* (rock).

The idea of a *pier* being a landing place for vessels in a harbour dates to the 1450s.

The older idea of a *pier* being the underpinning of a bridge is still used ashore, for example in walls and gates.

Pontoon

A *pontoon* is always a floating item but it may be a boat, a boat-plane, a bridge, or a floating jetty, and that's before we reach card games and villages.

The boat meaning in the oldest and dates to the 1300s and the Old French word *ponton* (a flat-bottomed boat). Later (1670s) it described the use of such boats to ford rivers and to support bridges but a formal *pontoon bridge* only arrived in 1778.

There are two versions of *pontoon* as a card game, both of them variants of blackjack.

The lakeside village of *Pontoon* in Mayo, Ireland is unrelated to *pontoon* boats or bridges. Its name is a corruption of the Irish for River Point. By sheer coincidence it's a popular spot with fishermen.

Port & Portugal

Port is a multi-functional word on ships.

Firstly, we use *port* as a word for a harbour. This was an Old English word from Latin via French drawn from *portus* (passage or entrance). Harbours were seen as doorways - where you left land to take to the sea, a different realm.

Portholes are discussed the Parts of a Ship chapter but again there are doors in their history.

The *port side* of a ship is the left (as you're looking at the prow, or front of the boat) and it arose in the 1540s to avoid confusion. The original term was larboard but it was too easily confused with starboard (the right, and opposite side of the boat). Dropping larboard in favour of port was made official in the U.S. Navy in 1846 and in the Royal Navy in 1844.

Larboard was used from the 1580s but it entered Middle English as *ladde-borde* in the early 1300s from *lade* (to load) and *bord* (side of a boat) – so it was the side of the boat for loading goods. There's also *hlada board* (loading side) in Norse so *larboard* was probably a Viking donation to English.

The phrase *any port in a storm* was first used in 1749.

The idea of *portage* was also related to boats, in this case canoes in Canada, which would be carried past rapids and then replaced in rivers for further progress. In this case the *port* was from Old French *porter* (to carry).

The final watery reference to *port* is another fluid entirely, one transported by ship. The fortified wine *port* (1690s) is named after the town of *Oporto* in Portugal which is a centre of *port* production to this day. *Oporto's* name translates as *The Port*, which neatly brings us back to the first meaning of *port* as it pertains to ships. *Portugal* itself is originally named for the *Port of Cale*, with thanks to invading Romans renaming the area.

Quay

Quay (1690s) is pronounced key – another tricky word to distinguish landlubbers from salty sea dogs.

Quay comes to English from the Middle English words *key, keye*, and *caye* - all meaning wharf. Thanks to the influence of French spelling *quai* we ended up with *quay* in English. *Quai* meant sandbank and has links to Celtic and Gaulish via words for wickerwork and fences which suggests early *quays* were river banks with additional fencing supports to provide a stable landing place for boats.

The word *key* meaning wharf comes from Old French *kai* (sandbank), not *quay*, despite the similar pronunciation and same linguistic roots. It's this origin that gives us the *Florida Keys*.

Wharf

A *wharf* is a level quay or pier to which a ship may tie up in order to load or unload.

Wharf entered English via the Old English word *hwearf* (shore or bank where ships can tie up) so the meaning was clear from the very beginning. Old English also had *hwearfian* (to turn) from Old Norse *hverfa* (to turn around) so this may be another seafaring term English borrowed from the Vikings.

The idea of a *wharf rat* (1836), somebody who hangs around docks evolved from actual rats.

A *wharfinger* arose as an English word in the 1500s with roots in *wharfage* (provision or accommodation at wharves) but this time meaning somebody who operates or manages a *wharf*. This term isn't used much now, having been replaced by harbourmaster.

The port city of Antwerp in Belgium is a compound word from *hand* and *wharf* (*werpum* in German).

11. Sails

All other Parts of a Ship are in that chapter, but sail names are so creative they demanded their own chapter. From *skyscraper* to *gollywobbler* they've billowed above us and found spaces in the English language, often to the point where landlubbers have no idea they once filled with wind and powered the exploration of the world.

Sails developed over time to drive ships further and faster. Clippers travelled at 17 knots where large warships of earlier times could only make 8-10 knots. Larger ships required larger *sails* but it was found that the resultant strain caused large *sails* to split so smaller *sails* in greater numbers were deployed instead, with more *sailors* on the crew to manage them.

Sailors were assigned to specific *sails*. Younger men were assigned to the tops while older, experienced *sailors* might reef the mainsails from the decks. Having more small *sails* reduced the damage a ripped *sail* from a cannon ball would do to the ship's speed as there would be plenty more *sails* intact. It also made replacing *sails* easier.

Sails were given names to indicate their position on the mast. The lowest were called the course, then moving up the mast you found the *top sail*, the *topgallant* and then the *royal*. Then the *sail* gained a further name based on which mast it was attached to – the *mizzen royal* was rigged from the *mizzenmast*, for example.

For more wind-catching the captain might order more *sails* on the outer edge of existing *sails*, these were *studding sails* so you'd get the *mizzen royal studding sail*. Naming all the *sails* on a clipper takes practice and this isn't a *sailing* manual so not all are covered here, but the more eccentric names begged to be included, especially as some of them have *sailed* into everyday English.

Cloud Cleaver

This particular *sail* is an imaginary one, no doubt inspired by the fanciful names given to certain *sails* on the tall ships. The *cloud cleaver* was rumoured (1883) to be carried by yankee ships, presumably to cut through the clouds themselves to gain speed.

Crack On

The contemporary meaning of this phrase is in flux. Some use *crack on* in a disbelieving fashion implying "get away with your nonsense" while in Australia the meaning has amorous overtones from wooing to bedroom activities.

The original meaning of *crack on* was to carry the full load of *sails* possible for a ship in order to make rapid progress. When the ship was in this state the *sails* and the ropes controlling them would make a sharp *cracking* noise.

Crack has several associations with speed. *Get cracking* means to work fast. *Crack shot* and other adjective uses of *crack* are often associated with quick work. *Crack* itself is likely to have been formed as a copy of the sharp, loud sound it describes.

Flying Jib

The *flying jib* is an extra sail on the outside of the *jib* on an extension of the jib-boom. As a landlubber I think that means it's *jib+.*

The *flying jib* dates from the 1600s and it comes from *flying* in the sense of being attached but allowing freedom of movement which sounds counter-intuitive until you think of *flying a flag.* Yes, it's attached to the flag pole (or *jib-boom*) but the rest of it is free to *fly.*

The idea of *flying* as being a way to describe rapid movement arrived in English around the same time, so this sail is associated with increased sailing speeds.

Footloose

The   bottom of a sail is called its *foot* and if it's not attached to the boom then it's *loose-footed*, dancing in the wind.

Footloose is a compound word of *foot* and *loose* from the 1690s which meant you were free to move your feet, you were unshackled. The idea of freedom to act as you pleased only arose in the late 1800s and by the time of the classic dance movie *"Footloose"* in 1984 starring Kevin Bacon as a teen new to a town where dancing and rock music have been banned, the association with sailing had been forgotten and replaced with freedom and dancing.

The film was loosely (*footloosely?*) based on true events in a small community in Oklahoma.

Furl

A landlubber may *furl*, or *unfurl* their umbrella or a flag, but a sailor is more likely to *furl* their sails and that's where the word came from.

Furling was the method of stowing the large volumes of canvas sails when not required. Sails were *furled* neatly into a bound roll against their wooden spar (as a flag is *furled* against its flagpole).

Furl entered English in the 1500s and its roots are debated. It may have been from a compounding of Latin *fer* (firm or support) and *lier* (to bind) and then via Middle French *ferler* (to *furl*) and Old French *ferliier* (tie up) or it could come from a shortening of *furdle* (to fold).

Gollywobbler

The *gollywobbler* is a "large square staysail hoisted between the masts of a schooner in a reaching wind to increase speed", but what's a staysail?

A staysail is a fore and aft sail set on lines that run diagonally downward from a mast. These lines (ropes) are called stays, hence the name. Unlike the square-rigged sails on a schooner, stay-lines are in line with the keel of the boat, i.e. at right angles to the rest of the sails. They catch wind from other directions and increase the ship's speed. A reaching wind comes side-on to the boat and staysails are perfectly positioned to use it.

Gollywobblers are still used on sailing boats today and there's even a series of wines named after them.

The linguistic origin of *gollywobbler* is sadly unknown, but I imagine that running aloft to hoist one would have been a *wobbly* and rather terrifying task on the taller of the tall-ships. The *gollywobbler* is believed to have given rise to the expression *I have the collywobbles* which means to be afraid.

Jib

A *jib* sail is a large, triangular foresail (one at the front) of a ship and has been part of the English language since the 1600s. *Jib's* origins are a little hazy. It was spelled *gibb* at first. That led to the sail being compared to a *gibbet* because of how it hung from the masthead, but that applies to many sails, not just the *jib*. Dutch has a couple of words which may have provided inspiration – *gijben* (to turn sails suddenly) and *gijk* (boom or spar on a sailing ship).

Jib gives us a nautical-to-fashion crossover where someone likes *the cut of your jib*. This came from sailors judging the quality of the seamanship on an approaching ship by assessing the condition of her *jibs*. The exact shape (or *cut*) of a *jib* sail at that time would also give a strong clue as to the nationality of a ship from a long distance, and a useful indication as to whether the ship was friend or foe.

Jib of Jibs

According to Admiral Smyth only flying kite men (see kites, below) knew this particular sail. It was the sixth *jib* (see *jib*, above) on the bowsprit, the last in a sequence that went like this – *storm jib, inner jib, outer jib, flying jib, spindle jib*, and finally *jib of jibs*.

Try saying that list after you've had your daily grog allowance.

Jigger

A *jigger* sail is set from the shorter mast located at the stern of a ketch or yawl sailing ship.

A *jigger* is also 1.5 ounce shot glass, a term which entered American English in 1836. The word *jigger* was also used (1824) to describe an illegal distillery. It's possible the word *jigger* to describe a small, but strong, drink arose from the *chigger* (1726) – a tiny mite or flea.

Kites

The *kite* sails were the highest and lightest sails on a tall ship, set above the royals. They included the *skysails, moonsails,* and *stargazers*. They are also known as *royal studding* or *topgallant studding sails*.

It's unclear if toy *kites* (1660s), or *kite sails* came first, but both are likely to be named for the *kite bird* – a type of European hawk whose name in Old English was *cyta*, in imitation of its cry. *Kites* hunt on the wing, soaring high like the sails.

Lug Sail

A *lug sail* is a fore and aft rigged, four cornered (but not square) sail suspended from a spar (or yard). A dipping *lug* can be partially lowered to be moved to the lee-side to help in tacking. It's still popular on small homemade wooden boats.

The *lug sail* evolved from square sails to improve how closely a ship can sail into the wind. Some believe the *lug* was the transitional step between square and lanteen style rigging. There are depictions of *lug* rigged boats in India dating back to the 6th century.

The origin of the name *lug sail* is debatable. Some sources believe it is so called in reference to the ear or jug handle (for which *lug* was slang in the 1620s) because of a physical resemblance to the way the sail draped. Others think it's because it was easily *lugged* or hoisted into position. The last group think it's because of the type of vessel the *lug* was used on, a *lugger*, which is close to the Dutch *logger* (slow ship). It's that last meaning that is also caught in the English verb *lug* – to move something slowly and with great effort.

Luff, Aluf, and Aloof

Luff or *luffing* is when a sailing sheet is eased too much and the airflow over the surface of the sail is disrupted. The *luff* is the leading edge of a sail. The leech (or leach) is the back edge. *Luff* (or *loof* as it is also spelled) is the windward side of a ship.

Luff, or *loof*, is likely to have come from Dutch sources, either Middle Dutch *lof* (windward side of a boat) or Dutch *loef*.

Luff gives us the idea of being *aloof* in withdrawn solitude from 1600s. A captain would give the order for the ship to *stay aloof*, meaning that they'd keep the ship's head into the wind in view of land but out of reach. This gradually became a way of describing a person who behaved that way.

Moonraker

The *moonraker sail*, also known as a *moonsail, hopesail*, or *hope-in-heaven*, is a square sail flown immediately above the skysail on the royal masts of a square-rigged sailing ship. It's a relatively unusual sail which would only be rigged on a ship built primarily for speed.

Moonraker is also the title of the third James Bond novel published by Ian Fleming in 1955 and featuring a plot about a missile called the *moonraker*. Its plot was later adapted (and considerably changed) to create the eleventh James Bond movie, featuring Roger Moore in the title role.

Reef and Reefer

To *reef* sails is to shorten them by partially tying them up. This is done to slow the ship's speed, when coming in to a harbour or to prevent strain on the sails in strong winds.

The idea of a *reefed* sail comes to English from the Vikings. Old Norse has the word *rif* (*reef* of sail) and it donated that to German (*reff*), Swedish (*ref*), Norwegian (*riv*), Danish (*reb*), as well as *reef* in English by the 1300s. By the 1660s it was being used as a verb to describe the action of taking in or rolling up part of a sail on a ship.

The use of *reef* to describe a coral area in the sea arose in the 1700s and may have been inspired by its long and apparently folded structures when viewed by shipboard explorers.

Reefer was first used in a nautical sense. In the 1800s, he was the midshipman responsible for *reefing* in the topsails, so clearly someone with an excellent head for heights. By the 1920s, *reefer* had a new meaning as a marijuana cigarette, or one who smoked them (with a head for highs, rather than heights), thanks to its resemblance to a rolled up sail.

Royal Sail

A *royal sail*, or *topgallant royal sail*, is a small sail flown above the topgallant (see below) on square-rigged sailing ships when their masts are tall enough for them to do so. Royals were introduced in the late 1600s.

Royal entered English in the mid 1200s as an adjective to describe something as literally being "fit for a king", although there's no evidence to connect the *royal sail* to *royalty* except in the sense that it flew at the top (or near the top – see skyscraper, skysail, and moonsail) of the mast.

Royal came to English from Latin *rex* (king) via *roial* (*royal* or *regal*) in Old French but the root word for *rex* was *reg* which means to move in a straight line or to direct in a straight line. Was the main job of a king to direct their people to stay in line? This concept neatly links *rulers* in both a regal and a line-drawing tool sense. Not something to mention at a *royal* garden party but one to ponder the next time you draw a straight line on a page.

Skysail

The *skysail* is the uppermost sail on either the main mast or royal mast, or both. Flown only in light winds, when trying to catch every scrap of wind possible, the *skysail* flew above the royal (topgallant) sail, but below a moonsail if one was used.

Skyscraper

Before *skyscrapers* became tall buildings (1888, American English) or very tall men (1857), they were associated with speed. A famous racehorse was thus named in the late 1700s.

The first use of *skyscraper* appears to have in the top rigging of sailing vessels. The *skyscraper* was a light sail carried rarely, and rigged so high that it appeared to be *scraping* the *sky* itself.

Other names for the highest sails were moonrakers or moonsails (see above), angel's foot stools, and stargazers. They were all used in dead calm conditions as they would rip away in stronger winds.

Spanker

A *spanker* sail (1794) comes from a changeable word root. *Spanking* originally (1660s) described something as being big and fine, particularly in reference to horses. Then as moving at a lively pace (1738) and in 1751 as something striking in times of size and impressiveness. So, throughout its early history to say something was a *spanker* was a positive thing, unrelated to any physical blow (that idea only entered English in 1854).

A *spanker* sail is a fore and aft sail set from the aft of the aftmost (furthest to the rear) mast on a square-rigged sailing ship. It was a large sail, relative to the other square-rigged sails. Given that it was large and impressive, that's probably why it was called a *spanker*.

Spinnaker

The *spinnaker* is a large triangular sail used on yachts when they've the wind with them to get extra speed. It billows out at the front and is often brightly coloured or covered in logos on modern racing yachts.

This sail was first used in 1866 on *The Sphinx*, an English cutter ship. The sail became known as *Sphinx' acre* because it was so large and the term gradually evolved through mispronunciation into *spinnaker*.

Taken Aback
{with thanks to Peter Sheehan}

To be *taken aback* (1792) is to be surprised by the sudden turn of events. The idea originated with ships rather than people.

The sails (particularly square-rigged sails) of a ship are *aback* when the wind blows them flat against the mast and spars which support them (1627). This problem generally causes all forward motion of the vessel to cease abruptly, a little like a person who is *taken aback* may stall in motion, speech, or thought.

By 1842 the expression was popular enough for Charles Dickens to use it in his "American Notes" book.

Three Sheets to the Wind
{with thanks to Peter Sheehan & Rick Ellrod}

If you're *three sheets to the wind* (or *in the wind* as the phrase started) then you are very drunk. Now, despite songs about drunken sailors this one relates to the sails rather than the crew.

First the term *sheet* needs to be defined for landlubbers. A *sheet* is the rope (or sometimes chain) fixed to the lower corners of a sail to keep it in place. If *three* of these vital *sheet* ropes are loose then the sail will flap about and the ship will lurch on its course.

The phrase was first seen in print in 1824 and there was a sliding scale of drunkenness. Tipsy was *one sheet in the wind, two sheets in the wind* (1815) was getting on a bit, but *three sheets* described somebody who could barely keep upright thanks to the effects of the grog they'd quaffed.

Topgallant

On a square-rigged sailing ship the *topgallant* is the square-rigged sail above the topsail. *Topgallant* is one of those words sailors enjoyed shortening to trick landlubbers. It's pronounced *t'gallant* or for the full term *topgallant sail* you get *t'garns'l*. Yes, really.

Later, rigging evolved to spilt the *topgallant* into an upper and lower *topgallant* for better handling.

Gallant entered English in the mid 1400s as meaning showy, finely dressed, lively, and merry. All earlier versions of the word in Old French spring from the idea of merriment and the concept of *gallantry*. The sail being named *gallant* is more likely to relate to putting on a good show of rigging, to increase speed to a lively pace, rather than any idea of courtesy.

The *topgallant* sail has contributed its name to the world map.

On the 13th of February 1802 Captain Matthew Flinders discovered an island group in South Australia off the

Eyre Peninsula and named them the *Topgallant Islands*, due to their resemblance to a ship under sail. They have enjoyed protected wilderness status since the 1960s to protect their flora and fauna including sea eagles and kestrels.

Flinders was a navigator and cartographer who led the first circumnavigation of Australia, identified it as a continent, and was imprisoned on Mauritius for six years on his way back to Britain despite claiming his scientific work should exempt him from the British-French war in progress at the time.

Yard & Yardarm

A *yard* in sailing terms isn't a distance or a garden, it's the wooden spar sticking out horizontally from the mast from which sails, particularly square sails, are set. Traditionally made of wood *yards* are also created from steel and carbon fibre. The *yard* is subdivided into sections, of which the *yardarms* are the tips furthest from the mast.

The expression *the sun is over the yardarm* arose from sailing in the North Atlantic when the sun would typically be above a specific *yardarm* by around eleven o'clock and the first tot of rum would be distributed to the crew. The phrase was first seen in print in the 1800s and is still used today as an excuse for an early alcoholic drink.

Yard was first used in Anglo-Saxon times to be a measure of about five metres of land (later renamed rod, pole, or perch). The idea of a *yard* being three feet long (36 inches) came about in the late 1300s and a rough equivalent would have been the ell (45 inches). *Yard* was sometimes used as Middle English slang for penis, a bit optimistic there.

The word *yard* came to Old English from *gerd* (Mercia) and *gierd* (West Saxon) and described a rod, staff, or measuring stick so presumably there was a long stick used to measure out land or cloth one *yard* at a time. Several other languages of the region and time had similar words.

A *yard* being a garden or patch of ground around a building, or indeed a *shipyard* (1700) came from different roots and the American English *yard sale* was first recorded in 1976.

12. Scurvy Pirates

The Golden Age of Piracy lasted from the 1650s to the 1730s, but of course piracy, on the high seas and ashore, persists to this day. During the golden age the number of pirates exploded thanks to increased trade of valuable goods in the triangular trade between Europe to Africa, on to the Caribbean, and back to Europe.

An amazing amount of pirate folklore is completely incorrect. Fiction and movies have a case to answer. Pirates almost never made anybody *walk the plank* (see below). They didn't keep parrots either, although they were valuable cargo during the period.

Despite being floating thieves, pirates have carved a romantic soft spot in many hearts so if you'd like to excel on the next Talk Like a Pirate Day (19th of September every year), or you'd simply like to embrace a *cutlass*-wielding, *scurvy*-ridden lifestyle, read on.

Note – the famous *Jolly Roger* is covered in the Flying the Flag chapter.

Avast!

Anybody who likes a good pirate yarn of swashbuckling and booty will be familiar with the exclamation *Avast, me hearties!* Probably no self-respecting pirates ever uttered the words but I love it all the same and am happy to repeat it on International Talk Like A Pirate Day (19th of September, mark your diaries, mateys!).

Only when finally reading "Moby Dick" did I discover it isn't a general yell of an over-excited buccaneer but a nautical order to stop and await further instructions. *Avast* is still used in sail-training and hence is in modern use despite its archaic sound.

The word's first usage was in 1681 and probably from *huod vast* or *hou'vast*, the Dutch for *hold fast*. When called out the sailor stops work and holds fast onto the nearest rope until they get further orders. Other sources claim *avast* is a corruption of the Italian interjection *basta* (enough/stop that).

Avast is a handy word for containing boisterous young humans. Early childhood educators and parents should adopt it immediately. An eye-patch and cutlass as props are recommended.

Bandana

Bandana comes to English from Hindi, possibly via Portuguese. The word *badnu* (or *bandhnu*) describes a dying technique similar to tie-dye where the cloth is knotted to create patterns on the finished fabric.

Pirate films would have us believe that those scurvy dogs regularly tied back their hair with a *bandana* but this is Hollywood flourish. Records, where they exist, describe pirates wearing tight fitting leather, woollen, or cloth caps which wouldn't blow away in the wind to protect themselves from the strong Caribbean sunshine.

They may have worn *bandanas* around their necks as a small scarf. But *bandanas* aren't mentioned as head gear and pirates weren't illustrated with them until the 1800s.

Booty

Booty is an obsession with fictional pirates but the practice of *booty* was more widespread and legitimate than you might expect.

When a ship was captured the rule of *booty* said you could take anything portable on or above the main deck. This was allowed in the British Royal Navy until after the Napoleonic Wars (1803-1815).

Cynical observers noted that while the ordinary sailors were busy on the main deck the officers would be below in the cargo holds dividing the more valuable spoils. All the major dictionaries are quick to point out that *booty* was stolen property, regardless of any "spoils of war" justification.

Booty entered English in the mid 1400s. It may come from an Old Norse word *btyi* (with the same meaning) or from Old French *boutin* (same meaning) in the 1300s.

In more recent times the idea of a *booty call* and *bootylicious* have come from this word and the idea of precious treasure. *Booty* referring to the female body is older than you might guess. It became African-American slang as early as the 1920s.

Buccaneer

Caribbean *buccaneers* were privateers in the 1700s and 1800s. A privateer was a legal pirate. They carried *letters of marque* entitling them to attack and capture ships of enemy forces. They weren't the official navy but their targets were, or were meant to be, the enemies of their patron country. Several of the major European nations employed privateers during the Age of Sail.

Apart from licensing thieves to supplement their fleet the countries also ran the risk of the privateers being bought by the highest bidder or simply doing as they wished once out of sight of the commissioning country. Did that happen? Yes, many times.

Equally, *letters of marque* weren't always honoured by the issuing nation. Captain Kidd had *letters of marque* and they hanged him anyway.

As for the word *buccaneer*, it has an unexpected link to *barbeques* (BBQs if you prefer) and *jerky*. Caribbean locals on Tortuga and Hispaniola (now Haiti and the Dominican Republic) dried meat on a frame called a *bocan* over a low fire. When the Spanish arrived in the area they loved the idea but called it a *barbacoa*, from which we get *barbeque*. The meat produced by this method they called *charque,* and we now call it jerky.

The sailors adopting this method of cooking/preserving meat for their ships became known as *buccaneers* as a result. In more modern times a *buccaneer* is typically found in the business realm acting in a reckless fashion.

Corsair

A *corsair* was a pirate, particularly along the Barbary Coast (from Egypt to the Atlantic). They operated along the North African Mediterranean coasts between the 1500 and 1800s. The Saracen and Turkish *corsairs* sometimes targeted their attacks against Christian ships, while the Christian *corsairs* (also known as Maltese *corsairs*) took their orders from the Knights of Saint John to attack the Turks.

The word *corsair* entered English in the early 1500s to mean a government-sanctioned pirate from the Middle

French word *corsaire* which came from the Provençal term *cursar* and Italian *corsaro*. Before that we had *cursarius* (pirate) in Medieval Latin and *cursus* (a running course) in Latin. The idea being that a run or journey transformed into an expedition seeking booty.

The *corsairs* didn't limit their area of operations to the Med, as evidenced by the 1631 sack of Baltimore in Cork, Ireland by *corsairs* from Algeria. The small village was put to the torch and more than 100 men, women, and children prisoners were taken as galley slaves. The vast majority of them never returned.

Cutlass

The *cutlass* was a short, heavy sword (or large knife) with a slightly curved blade with one cutting edge. The handle was usually covered with a basket guard to protect the hand. Although generally a short sword, some Caribbean *cutlasses* were up to three feet (91cm) in length. It was used more for cutting and slashing than for thrusting.

Linguistically *Cutlass* is unrelated to *cut*. *Cutlass* came into English in the late 1500s from an original Latin root of *cultellus* (a small knife), the smaller form of *culter* (knife or ploughshare).

Although also used on land, the *cutlass* became the weapon of choice for all sailors, not just pirates, as it was cheap to make, required very little training, and as a cutting weapon is more effective than a thrusting blade like a rapier, against enemies not wearing armour.

Sailors didn't wear armour as a) it's too bulky for their work and b) if you fall overboard you're going to sink, fast. The *cutlass'* shorter length was better for close combat on deck.

The legend goes that pirates would swing across on ropes from their ship to their prey with knives clenched in their teeth and that's where we get *armed to the teeth* but sadly there's little evidence to support it.

Cutlass drill was introduced in the Royal Navy in 1814 and retained until 1936 although there are reports of some servicemen carrying them during World War II. The last usage of the weapon was probably when sailors from the *HMS Cossack* boarded the *Altmark* in 1940 to liberate British prisoners of war.

Doubloon

The *doubloon* so beloved by pirates in their treasure chests was a Spanish gold coin made from 22 carat gold and minted from the 1500s to the 1700s in Spain, and its colonies. The term, which comes from the Spanish word *doblón* (double), came about either because it was worth two ducats or because of the *double* portrait of the Spanish ruling couple Ferdinand and Isabella.

The *doblón* word itself came from Latin *duplus* (twofold, twice as much) which also gives us *duo* and *duplicitous*.

Filibuster

Filibuster is one of those words which connects two very different concepts.

Filibuster joined English at the end of the 1700s direct from the Dutch word *vrijbuiter* (*freebooter*). The *freebooters* weren't seeking free footwear but actually looking for free plunder or *booty* (see above). The idea of a *freebooter* or a *filibuster* was that of a *privateer* in the West Indies (as discussed in *buccaneer*, see above) who sometimes blockaded islands.

During 1850-1858 a *filibuster* came to mean a specific type of *privateer*, the privately funded American troops blockading Latin countries like Cuba, Mexico, and Nicaragua. These military adventurers were effectively land pirates attempting to overthrow Central American governments for private gain.

By 1865 it was a short jump from blockading nations to overthrow authority to the idea of blockading legislation and defying authority in the United States Senate. The rules permit a senator, or series of senators, to speak for as long as they wish on a topic of their choice. This can be used to block voting on proposed legislation and hence delay it. Rule changes over the years have limited the effectiveness of such a move but it can still produce results when deployed close to an important deadline such as a Senate recess or a government shutdown deadline.

The longest *filibustering* speech was given over the course of 24 hours and 18 minutes by James Strom Thurmond from South Carolina in 1957 in a desperate effort to delay the Civil Rights Bill. He did not prevent the bill passing into law. He did however manage to keep it quiet that he'd fathered a daughter with his African-American maid who was only 16 at the time.

Give No Quarter

If a pirate ship flew a red flag it meant that *no quarter* would be given to their prey i.e. they wouldn't spare the lives of captives.

Giving no quarter has been illegal in war since the Hague Convention of 1907.

The red flag has been used, rarely, in military situations ashore. Santa Anna flew one from the church bell tower to show the rebels in the Alamo that he would *give no quarter*. It is unclear if *giving no quarter* arose with combatants afloat or on land

The origin of *quarter* in this case is disputed. Either it comes from a commander ordering that they wouldn't house, or *quarter*, captured enemies (and hence they all had to be killed) or *quarter* means relationship or agreement (a meaning in use around 1600) so *no quarter* means you weren't going to negotiate with your enemies. The former seems most likely.

Peg leg

This nickname for sailors who had lost a leg in battle or accident at sea isn't the most politically correct, but would have been used very rarely in real life no matter what pirate movies would have us believe.

Most sailors in the Age of Sail who lost a leg would have died of infection shortly thereafter in an era before antibiotics or knowledge of germs. There were exceptions to this rule, but not many.

Fictional *peg legs* are vastly more common. Perhaps the most famous is Captain Ahab in "Moby Dick" who had an ivory prosthetic. Long John Silver is nearly always depicted as having a wooden leg but in the book "Treasure Island" by Robert Louis Stevenson he is described as using crutches and no artificial leg is ever mentioned.

Pieces of Eight

For this coin, a popular pirate currency, you need to think about pizza, and specifically how you cut one into slices. Pieces of eight were silver Spanish coins worth one *peso* or eight *reales*. Sometimes they were cut up in *eight* individual *pieces*, all worth a single *reale*.

Pieces of eight were the world's first global currency, used both within the vast Spanish Empire of the 1600s but also outside it. The silver for the coins came from the mountains of Bolivia, at great human cost to the locals and to African slaves.

Pieces of eight were legal tender in the United States until 1857.

Pirate

Theft is one of the oldest crimes so it is unsurprising that *pirate* is one of the oldest words in this book. *Pirate* entered English in the 1200s and even became a surname. Occupations often became surnames at that time, think of Cooper, Taylor, Smith – still common surnames.

Piracy was, and is, a risky business with potentially large rewards and that's where the word came from. The old root verb *per* means to try or risk something. This gave us *peira* as a noun for a try or an attack in Greek. From *peira* you got *peirates* for a person who attacks ships, a brigand or *pirate*. *Peirates* spread to German *Pirat*, Dutch *piraat*, Italian and Spanish *pirata*, and Latin *pirata* for a corsair or sea robber. The hop into English *pirate* was easy.

Pirates don't always seize the same kind of booty. By 1701 a *pirate* had become somebody who took another's work without permission. By 1913 *pirates* had moved into broadcasting with the rise of *pirate* radio stations who played their music without official licenses. Copyright and software *piracy* is still a major issue worldwide.

Privateer

Privateers were state-sponsored pirates. They were given letters of marque but sailed in their own private ships. Their targets were their state's enemy shipping and they kept most plunder they seized. By the 1700s there were thousands such *privateers*, for various countries, in the Caribbean but with the end of the Spanish War of Succession their letters of marque were withdrawn and many turned to regular piracy.

Henry Morgan was one of the most successful *privateers* but others included Francis Drake and John Hawkins. *Privateering* was outlawed formally in 1856.

Salmagundi

A *salmagundi* is a mish-mash of a dish dating from the 1600s which was never exactly the same any time it was made.

The chef could include anything – meat, fish, edible flowers, eggs, fruit, nuts. These cold ingredients, whatever you had available, would be topped with a spicy dressing and your dish was complete. Apparently pirates loved it.

See also the *Salmagundi* chapter.

Scurvy

Scurvy can affect any sailor, or malnourished landlubber, but with the prevalence of phrases like *scurvy knaves*, *scurvy pirates*, and *ye scurvy dogs* the word fitted best here.

Scurvy, a disease caused by a deficiency of vitamin C, has symptoms including fatigue, sore limbs, and weakness but as it advances issues include gum disease, losing teeth, and bleeding from the skin.

Sailors on long voyages often went short on fresh fruit and vegetables. In an era before canning and refrigeration, *scurvy* was rife aboard ships and a leading cause of death amongst crew.

The word *scurvy* entered English in the 1560s as a variant of the adjective *scurfy* used to describe someone who is diseased or covered with scabs. Knowledge of the disease was widespread throughout history with ancient Greeks and Egyptians being aware of it.

Sadly, the association with fresh fruit as a cure was discovered, used, and lost repeatedly throughout history. Orange and lemons were noted as a cure by Captain Richard Hawkins in 1593. Daily orange juice was noted by John Woodall in 1636. Dr. James Lind established vitamin C as the cure in 1747.

From 1795 British warships were required to carry lime juice to prevent *scurvy*. American sailors still call British sailors limeys as a result. Tragically the practice was only formally adopted by the merchant navy in 1854. It is estimated that 800,000 British seaman died needlessly of *scurvy*.

During the Age of Exploration the Portuguese planted fruit trees and vegetables on the island of Saint Helena (later prison to Napoleon) in the south Atlantic Ocean. The island was their stopping point on voyages between Europe and Asia. They left their sick there to recover and resume their voyage on the next ship.

See *gimlette* in the Eponym chapter for more information on how limes were introduced to help this issue in the Royal Navy.

Shiver Me Timbers

Robert Louis Stevenson gave us one of the best fictional pirates in old Long John Silver in "Treasure Island" (1883) and several times during the book Long John swore using the expression *shiver me timbers*, but Stevenson didn't invent the phrase. It appeared in print fifty years earlier in another story.

An old meaning of *shiver* (largely unused now, although it does make sense if you've ever been cold enough to shiver violently) is to break into pieces. So if a sailor vows to let his *timbers* (his boat) *shiver* into pieces, he's serious.

There's a distinct chance that the expression was only ever used by melodramatic fictional pirates whose favourite subject in school was definitely aaaaaaarrrrt (sorry, couldn't resist).

Walk the Plank

Walking the plank was a cruel method of execution where the victim was forced, hands tied and blindfolded, to walk a plank and jump into the sea to drown.

Walking the plank is a key part of pirate folklore and sadly it was a real thing but not often on pirate ships. It was used as an impromptu form of punishment at sea during the 1700 and 1800s.

The practice was defined in a 1788 dictionary as being "a mode of destroying devoted persons or officers in a mutiny on shipboard...by this means, as the mutineers suppose, avoiding the penalty of murder." Also in 1788, the former governor of Senegal, John Barnes, gave evidence to the British House of Commons (parliament) about the slave trade and in the course of his testimony mentioned the practice being used on slaves when rations ran short.

All credible reports happened *after* the main age of sailing ship pirates. None of the big names like Blackbeard, Henry Avery, or Henry Morgan used this method. Pirates usually ensured the survivors of their attacks were left on sacked ships or put ashore. They were only interested in the booty, not in mass murder. However they might stoop to it for disposing of rivals, often in the misguided belief that it didn't count as murder because the sea did their work for them.

Despite this, the world of cinema has given us many dramatic *walking the plank* moments in pirate movies, and even in George Lucas' "Star Wars – Return of the Jedi" without a drop of water in sight.

13. Maps & Navigation

While navigation on land can be tricky, an explorer with a compass could always rely on finding North and perhaps draw a map as they went, filling in the landmarks they found on the way.

Ship-based explorers had more difficulties to handle. Once out of sight of land they faced endless blue. Until the invention of reliable time-pieces they struggled to navigate, especially if bad weather hid the stars from view. There's a reason why old sailing charts often had random sea creatures inked in blank spaces. Vast sections of the oceans remained unexplored until recent times. The depths of the sea are the last great unexplored frontier on our planet.

Early seafaring explorers such as the Vikings risked their lives to find new lands, navigating with rudimentary tools and plenty of hope. Even Columbus had to cheat the locals on Jamaica with the use of an almanac and a lunar eclipse to convince them to help his crew on their fourth and final voyage.

This chapter takes a look at the navigation tools and words used afloat.

All at Sea

Navigation at sea has come a long way in the last century. With the advent of G.P.S. and increasingly sophisticated navigation aids it's becoming harder to get lost at sea. Before the advent of reliable compasses, detailed *charts* (see below), and other tools, the mariner who lost sight of land and was *all at sea* took a huge risk. There are good reasons why the Age of Exploration didn't explode until improved navigation tools enabled captains to be more certain of their position on the seas.

As a result if you were *all at sea* you were in danger of being lost, or at the very best deeply confused. This is the meaning which has persisted in modern English.

America

Clearly *America* the place existed before English and is a landmass rather than an ocean, but its name comes from the sea.

There is, however, some debate over which person gave their name to the continent.

The accepted winner is *Amerigo* Vespucci (1454-1512) the navigator, explorer, and cartographer from Florence, Italy. Around 1502 he demonstrated that Brazil and the West Indies were not the coast of Asia as initially thought by Columbus but were a new land mass, called the New World and later termed the *Americas* based on his name in Latin, *Americus*.

Another possible contender is Richard *Amerike* (1445-1503) who was a wealthy merchant trading from Bristol. The city of Bristol sent fishing vessels in search of cod to Newfoundland before Columbus' first voyage in 1492, possibly as early as 1480. They'd been forced to find a new fishing ground after the King of Denmark banned their fisheries and trade with Iceland.

This part of Newfoundland where the Bristol sailors were processing fish had been named Brassyle (probably a reference to the legendary island of Hy Brasil - see Old Sea Dog Yarns chapter). Richard *Amerike* shipped salt to there in 1481.

In 1495 Giovanni Cabot was authorised by King Henry VII of England to make a voyage of discovery to claim land in the New World in England's name. Cabot found investors and maps in Bristol. One of the investors was *Amerike* and his name was probably on Cabot's charts from his journey. Copies of those were sent to Spain, where Columbus and Vespucci probably used them too.

Regardless of which tale you believe, *America* was named for either a merchant trader or an ocean explorer.

Astrolabe

An *astrolabe* is a disc-shaped navigational tool used to measure the altitude of the sun and stars without a need for a visible horizon. The *astrolabe* was invented by the Greeks and refined by the Arabs. *Astrolabes* were used for ship navigation until the 1700s but didn't work in rough seas.

Astrolabe comes from the Greek *astrolabos organon* (star taking instrument) which is a compound of *astron* (star) and *lambanien* (to take). As you'd expect, *astron* also gives us *astronomy*.

Charts

When is a map not a map? When it's afloat. Never talk to a sailor about a map. They only use *charts*.

In fairness a nautical *chart* is somewhat different to a standard map. A nautical *chart* represents hydrographical data such as detailed water depths, shoreline, tide predictions, obstructions to navigation such as wrecks and rocks, and navigational aids like buoys, beacons, and lighthouses.

Chart has been in use as a map for ship's navigators since the 1570s in English. *Chart* has Latin roots with *charta* meaning paper, card, and map. It moved through Middle French as *charte* (card or map) until it reached English.

In the 1600s English had dual meanings for *chart* – either a map or a playing card, but over time the word card took over and left *chart* to the sea-farers.

The word *chart* gives us the idea of *uncharted waters* being dangerous as they could conceal unknown obstacles and problems. *Chart* sneaked its way into popular culture via *music charts*.

Cyber
{with thanks to ZZNewell on CritiqueCircle}

Cyber may not a word with obvious nautical roots but this word, technically a shortening of *cybernetics* (the study of communication and control systems in living beings and machines pioneered in the 1940s), has watery origins.

Cybernetic was formed from the Greek word *kubernetes* which means steersman, from *kubernan*, the verb to steer.

Once *cybernetics* was shortened to a prefixing *cyber-* it proliferated during the 1960s and up to the 1990s in words such as *cyborg* (*cyber* merged with *organism*), *cybermen* in Dr. Who, *cyberspace, cyberbullying*, and *cybercrime*.

Fairway

Golfers are more familiar with the *fairway* being shorter grass leading to a golf hole and the target for their drives, but the origin of the word is blue rather than green.

The golfing *fairway* arose in 1898 but is pre-dated by *fairway* meaning a navigational channel of a river or narrow bay in the 1580s. It is, as you might guess, a compound word formed by joining *fair* and *way*.

To Fathom Out Something

Depth is a key piece of knowledge for any navigator at sea. Bring your ship too close to a covered sandbar or reef and you'll find yourself aground, or worse.

That's where *fathoms* come in. A *fathom* is one of the old units of measurement. A *fathom* is the distance from fingertip to fingertip of a man's outstretched arms. Typically this is about six feet.

From the 1300s people who embraced each other with their arms around each other were said to be *fathoming*. *Fathoming out* in the 1500s meant to measure something using outstretched arms.

With time the idea of *fathoming* meant to get to the bottom of something or to take soundings about something. This arose from the practice of checking the water depth beneath a ship by using a weighted rope lowered into the water with knots tied at each *fathom*.

Getting to the bottom of something on dry land can be important, but if your ship didn't have enough *fathoms* beneath it, it could spell disaster and recording the *fathoms* on early charts was a vital aid to navigation.

Lodestar

A *lodestar* is a star by which you chart your course, usually the Pole Star. *Lodestar* is used figuratively as a guiding light, an inspiration on which your hopes are set. *Lodestar* was originally a surname in English, in the late 1200s but gained its meaning as a star that serves as a guide from the 1300s by joining *star* and *lode* together. *Lode* was a Middle English word for a way or course, something to be followed.

Similar words are found in Old Norse *leidarstjarna*, German *leitstern*, and Danish *ledestjerne*.

Longitude & Latitude

Longitude is the measure of the east-west distance of the surface of the earth (or dome of the sky) and comes directly to English from Latin *longitudo* (length, long duration) and *longus* (long). *Latitude* entered English at the same time (late 1300s) to measure breadth again from Latin, this time *latitudo* (width) from *latus* (wide, large).

Early geographers believed the known world to be bounded on the western side by the Atlantic Ocean and measured it from east to west rather than north to south. Because the world they knew was broader than it was deep they named the east west breadth of it the *longitudo* and the north south length of it they called the *latitudo*.

Now we have the vertical ones called *longitude* lines or meridians whereas the horizontals are *latitude* or parallels (parallel to the equator). The zero meridian is at Greenwich in London but before this was adopted universally the French measured from Paris and the Spanish measured from Tenerife or Cadiz.

To chart an accurate course or determine a precise location you need both. Early mariners were forced to cluster on well-known trade routes where they were vulnerable to attack.

Latitude was measured using a quadrant (see below) or astrolabe (see above) but *longitude* was a trickier problem to solve. Galileo Galilei thought he'd cracked it in 1612 by using the moons of Jupiter as a sort of universal clock but observations were too hard to take from the rolling deck of a ship.

In 1714 the British government offered a large reward for a solution to the issue at sea. In 1773 John Harrison, a self-taught clockmaker, claimed the reward for his marine chronometer but the lunar method persisted thereafter thanks to their expensive nature.

Mayday

When navigation skills go wrong, or you're using the map upside down, your ship may flounder. Then it's time to send a *mayday*.

Mayday is the international radio distress call for help when there's an immediate danger of loss of life, for example a ship that is sinking. It is used primarily by aviators and mariners.

Like other distress signals used on land, such as whistle blasts and piles of rocks, it is always transmitted in groups of three.

It originates from the French phrase *m-aidez* (help me) and is relatively modern.

Mayday originated in 1923 in Croydon, London. Frederick Stanley Mockford, a senior radio operator at Croydon airport, was asked to think of a word to indicate emergency that could be easily understood by pilots and ground staff. As most flights were between Croydon and Paris, he picked *m'aider* (short for *venez m'aider*- come and help me). In 1927 the voice call *mayday* on radio replaced the Morse Code SOS on telegraph as the standard distress call. Croydon Airport, replaced by London Heathrow, closed in 1959.

A false *mayday* call in the U.S.A. is punishable by up to six years in jail and/or a quarter of a million dollar fine.

Plain Sailing

Plain sailing nowadays indicates clear and steady progress.

However *plain sailing* comes from *plane sailing* where *plain* means simple and clear whereas *plane* means flat. That distinction is important but in the 1600s when the phrase arose, such differences were ignored. So *plain sailing* was originally coined not to describe easy voyages but the method of navigation used on voyages.

Plane sailing is a simplified form of navigation where the navigator ignores the curvature of the earth and charts their course as if the world were flat. This method, as you'd guess, made the calculations simpler than *Mercator's sailing* which took into account the curvature of the planet.

Gerardus Mercator (1512-1594) was a Flemish cartographer who gave us the word atlas for a collection of maps and the Mercator Projection as a way to represent a curved world map in two dimensions. This enabled mariners to chart courses over long distances without constant compass adjustments.

Plain came to English about 1300 via Old French *plain* (flat, smooth) from Latin *planus* (flat, level) and didn't get the additional meaning of simple for another century. *Plain English* wasn't used until 1500.

Quadrant

Originally used by astronomers, as were many shipboard navigation instruments, the *quadrant* (1400) gets its name from the Latin word *quad* (four) because the *quadrant* looks like a quarter of a circle rendered in brass.

Astronomers used it to calculate the angular height of a star or the sun. Surveyors used it to measure the height of a building, a mountain, or to calculate cannon ranges.

When sailors got their hands on one it was used to get the height of Polaris (the pole star, key in celestial navigation). The height of Polaris above the horizon varied with your latitude and hence could be used to set a course. This particular gem of information was key to the Age of Exploration and came from Arab sailors who'd had to learn to navigate out of sight of land to avoid dangerous shoals off the north and eastern coasts of Africa.

The *quadrant* did have some drawbacks. The worst was that using it involved staring at the sun, never a good move for your eyesight. Blindness was a peril for navigators. When a ship sails below the equator Polaris is no longer visible and the sun has to be used to determine latitude using a *quadrant*. This explains the prevalence of eye-patches amongst sailors, and pirates, of that period. They hadn't lost their eyes during sword fights and battles but thanks to staring at the sun for navigation purposes.

RADAR

RADAR stands for **RA**dio **D**irection **A**nd **R**ange and is an electronic method of locating objects using radio waves.

The major development of *RADAR* took place in the 1930s but it was based on the groundbreaking experiments on electromagnetic radiation by Heinrich Hertz in the 1880s, who was in turn working on theories from Scottish physicist James Clerk Maxwell.

Hertz's work was seen to have naval potential for detecting enemy ships by Christian Hülsmeyer, a German engineer. He established patents in several countries and demonstrated to the German navy without success.

The first observation of the *RADAR* effect was at the U.S. Naval Research Laboratory in Washington, D.C. in 1922 but despite this the U.S. Navy didn't bite either.

The principle of *RADAR* was rediscovered at that lab by L.A. Hyland in 1930 but it took until 1939 for its usefulness to be appreciated when installed on the *USS New York* battleship.

Throughout the late 1930s and World War Two, *RADAR* developed rapidly, particularly so in Germany, and primarily for detecting aircraft. After the war the developments continued and it's now used on board ships, in air traffic control, spacecraft, and for missile detection.

RADAR owes its name to American scientists. The British name choice was radiolocation.

To *be on someone's radar*, in the figurative sense, entered common speech in the 1950s.

Sextant

The *sextant* was a vital piece of navigation gear before the ease of G.P.S. (global positioning system). You may have seen one held to the captain's eye in a swashbuckling drama – a brass instrument that looks like a combination of a slice of brass pizza, a monocle, and a mini telescope.

The *sextant* (1620s) was used to determine your present latitude and the term is said to have been coined by Dutch astronomer Tycho Brahe from modern Latin *sextans* (a sixth) because it has a graduated arc equal in size to one sixth of a circle's circumference.

As discussed in Longitude and Latitude (above) getting your latitude was only half the battle but the *sextant* was standard navigation kit for centuries.

SONAR

This instrument for underwater detection was named from the first letters of **So**und **Na**vigation **A**nd **R**anging in 1946. It was called ASDIC originally and was one of the big inventions to come from World War Two. First installed in 1941 on a British warship, it enabled the hunt for enemy submarines.

Based on how long the detection ping took to travel back to the hunting warship the range could also be established.

SONAR is now used on some fishing trawlers to help them detect shoals of fish. It's also used to detect underwater obstacles and to improve maritime charts.

Bats and dolphins use their own versions of *SONAR* to navigate and find prey.

SOS

SOS entered English on the 1st of July 1908 as the international morse code distress signal, particularly for maritime use. The letters were chosen because they are easy to transmit and difficult to mis-read. One alternative suggestion was CQD – come quickly, distress. CQ is a general call to all ships and D was for danger. *SOS* is for telegraph signals only, the signal if speaking, on radio for example, is mayday (see above).

SOS entered German three years earlier and is not an initialisation of any series of words or phrase, but this doesn't stop people ascribing meanings to it. The various folk etymologies include; *Save our souls, send out succour, save our ship, sink or swim, same old stuff,* and my personal favourite - *stretch or starve* - good advice for a crowded dinner table.

Morse Code is an eponym, named for its inventor Samuel Morse (discussed in my earlier book "How To Get Your Name In The Dictionary"). It acquired the @ symbol in 2004 for email addresses. Its first update since World War I.

SOS is transmitted as . . . - - - . . .

SOS has entered common language to such an extent that it has given song titles to Abba and Rihanna, and even a popular TV programme, "*DIY SOS*", on the BBC.

Steerage

Steerage originally (early 1400s) referred to the steering mechanism of a ship and was a compound word of *steer* and *age* with *steer* being a word with Proto-Germanic roots for a *steering pole* or rudder.

As a result the *steerage area* was towards the rear of the ship where its *steering* was controlled by a large tiller which might protrude into the *steerage* compartment in the aft of the ship. In the 1800s the name was retained for the cheapest passenger accommodation which was often located in the same position below decks where the noise of the ship's engine was loudest and unceasing. Later called third class, there was little light or ventilation and passengers often had to do their own cooking and cleaning there.

Only 25% of the Titanic's *steerage* passengers survived, while 97% of first class female passengers survived.

Sunstones

Vikings navigated from the Baltic to Greenland, Iceland, and Newfoundland (which they called Vineland) using sundials. In those northerly seas overcast and foggy days caused issues for any sundial user.

To circumvent this the Vikings used *sunstones*, rock crystals, in those conditions. Recent research in the Arctic Ocean on the Swedish icebreaker *Oden* proved that *sunstones* such as cordierite, calcite, and tourmaline work like polarising filters and can pinpoint the position of the sun despite cloud cover. Fans of the TV series "Vikings" will have seen this method in action.

This method explains how the great seafarers managed such arduous journeys in an era before accurate charts and time pieces, many centuries before the Age of Exploration led by the Portuguese and Spanish fleets.

Tack

Tacking, from the 1550s, is to turn a boat's course into the wind at an angle, thus enabling it to make progress without the wind directly behind the sails. This comes from the word *tack* in a rigging sense – the ropes which moved a boat to one side of its normal course to take advantage of wind from the side. This use of *tack* gives us the expression to *take a new tack* (1670s) meaning to take a new approach from a fresh angle.

Tacking in boats is unrelated to *tack* describing food, horse's harness, or a *tack* being a type of nail. The nail *tack* is the oldest form c. 1400.

Time Ball

The *time ball* may no longer be used but it was a vital tool for mariners in the 1800s. This device, a large black ball mounted in an easily visible spot at major ports worldwide, was lowered exactly on the stroke of noon so ship's navigators could set their chronometers to the correct time. As discussed in longitude & latitude above, accurate time-keeping was vital for navigation out of sight of land.

There are about 60 *time balls* still in existence. You'll find them at Sydney Observatory, the Citadelle of Quebec, The Royal Greenwich Observatory, and at the Titanic Memorial in New York, amongst other places.

14. Sea Battles

In war, naval battles were as important as those fought on land. Sea battles have provided a surprising number of words and phrases to the English language.

Turning a blind eye and *clearing the decks* are more often found in offices now than on deck, while we associate *hot pursuit* with police chases. Who would guess that *jingoism* comes to the dictionary thanks to whalers from the Basque country?

Clear the Decks

Clearing the decks is an important task before a ship engages in battle. *Decks* were busy places with various jobs in progress at most times of day and night. When the captain ordered the *decks cleared* the crew would remove or fasten down any loose objects.

The phrase moved from the nautical realm into general use in the 1800s and is now most commonly used figuratively about clearing your desk, or mind, of small tasks before starting a new or more important project.

Close Quarters

During the 1600s there would often be a temporary partition or wooden blockhouse constructed on the deck of a ship. These wooden barriers were called *close-fights* or *close-quarters* with the meaning of *close* being linked to *closed* or shut, rather than nearby, but over time that distinction was lost.

If the ship was boarded during a battle some crew-members would hide in the blockhouse with their muskets and fire out of the *close-quarter* through loopholes to disperse the boarders.

This method of defence was *up close* fighting in comparison with using your cannons to blast an enemy ship. It was used at sea, and later on land, for many years.

From the early 1700s the phrase *close quarters* came to mean being in proximity to something or someone.

Cut and Run

Cut and run is now used to mean leaving with undue haste. You might *cut and run* when your least favourite relation arrives at a family party, for example.

In the 1600s *cut and run* was a sea ambush. The ship rode at anchor in a river, inlet, or small estuary in running water with sails furled but only lightly tied so quick *cuts* would allow them to fill with wind. Combined with the tug of the current a sailing ship could *run* into pursuit or attack at the first glimpse of an enemy ship.

This *cutting* didn't include *cutting* the anchor rope. The anchor was a piece of equipment no good captain would want to lose, unless forced to, and there would usually be time to weigh anchor while the sails were prepared.

The inclusion of *run* in the phrase adds an implication of cowardice and self-interest, but that was not original intent as the vessel *cutting and running* was in attack mode, not retreat.

Hot Pursuit

To be in *hot pursuit* of something is to make every effort to catch it. It's commonly applied to road chases of criminals by the police, but the phrase started on the seas.

In the 1400s pursuit on the ocean blue came in two temperatures – *hot* or *cold*. *Cold pursuit* (or *cold chase*) was a ship hunting down another in international waters but without seeing the pursued ship. The *hot pursuit* was the same chase but this time with a quarry ship in sight.

Although not written into law, it was common custom that in such cases the pursuing ship could follow its prey into a country's own waters to finish the job. *Hot pursuit* was only allowed if the chase could be proven to have begun in international waters and open seas. Otherwise it was a hostile act against that country.

Jingoism

Jingoism is a negative term for excessively aggressive patriotism leading to warlike rhetoric or foreign policy, but did you know it comes from whaling?

The Basques, from Europe, were one of the first peoples to put together organised whaling fleets and by the mid 1500s had established bases in Newfoundland and Nova Scotia. Their experience made them valuable recruits to the crews of other nations as they began whaling too.

The Basque language then seeped into English. *Bizarre* (bearded, referring to the Spanish with whom they were near permanently at war), *scimitar, tambourine,* and *sarsaparilla* were some of the linguistic acquisitions.

Jinko (God) led to the exclamation *By Jingo!* as another way of saying By God! and became a very popular expression in English.

During the Russian-Turkish War (1877-1878) anti-Russian sentiment ran high in Britain. When the quickest trade route to the British colony of India was threatened, Benjamin Disraeli (1804-1881), leader of the conservative government, wanted to send the British fleet into Turkish waters to protect British interests in the region. Their rallying song included the lines –

"We don't want to fight, but *by Jingo* if we do,
We've got the ships, we've got the men, and we've got the money too."

As a result they were nicknamed the *jingoists* and the phrase is now attached to anybody who is seen as promoting war in the name of national interests.

Panic Stations

Panic stations is a state of high alert, possibly even melodramatic over-reaction to minor events for comic effect.

The real *panic stations* was an order dating to naval battles during World War I. The Royal Navy had a few orders relating to stations (positions the crew had to attend when the order was given) such as action stations (when under attack) and *panic stations*.

The *panic stations* order would be given to crew on a Q ship but it wasn't intended to get the crew to *panic* in the face of an attack – quite the opposite. The crew would calmly go to their disguised gun positions and await the attack order.

The Q ships were used as tool by the Royal Navy against German U-boat submarines. The Q ships were disguised as old, rusting cargo ships (no threat to anybody) but they were actually heavily-armed military ships filled with wood and other buoyant cargo to help them float even after they'd taken a few hits. Once a U-boat had fired at the Q ship and it had been apparently half sunk or disabled, the U-boat would surface, at which time the crew (at their *panic stations*) could fire on the submarine with ease.

As for *panic*, its origins lie with the Greek pan-pipe playing nature god, *Pan*. Any unexplained noises in the forest might throw the unwary into a state of *panic*.

Regatta

A *regatta* is most commonly used today to describe a boat race and in that sense it dates to the 1700s in England, however the original *regatta* was a little earlier and took place in Venice, not Henley.

The first *regatta* took place in the 1650s and was a race between gondoliers on the Grand Canal. *Regatta* is a Venetian dialect word which translates as "contention for mastery" from the verb *rigattare*(compete or haggle).

The *regatta* still takes places on the first Sunday in September each year in Venice with events for various sizes of gondola, male and female teams and shorter races for children plus historical re-enactments and plenty of costumes and colourful decorations of the boats. Even with all the flourishes, the *regatta* is still a serious boat race and mastery is hotly contested.

Rostrum

A *rostrum* was originally the beak of Roman war galleys which was used to ram other vessels during battles. The *rostra* (plural of *rostrum*) of captured galleys (primarily from their victory over Antium in 338 B.C.) were brought home and displayed in front of the speaker's platform at the Forum in Rome. Over time it was renamed the *rostrum* as a result. The word entered English in 1766 as a platform for public speaking.

The word itself has roots in the verb *to gnaw*. Thankfully this does not apply to modern public speaking.

Shot Across the Bows

The *bow* is the front third, or shoulders, of a ship. *A shot across the bows* was the naval custom of firing a cannon there to show the enemy you were serious. It didn't damage the ship, which you might want to capture intact, but it would scare them. It would either result in the target ship stopping and raising a white flag, or commencing battle.

The idea *of a shot across the bows* being a warning entered general use in English during the 1930s.

Trident

A *trident* is a spear with three prongs. It's what you might see Neptune, or Aquaman, sporting in an illustration. The word dates to the 1400s and comes from Latin where *tri* means three and *dens* means tooth. It was also the name of a nuclear powered submarine created in the 1970s.

Turn a Blind Eye

The idea of deliberately ignoring something by *turning a blind eye* comes from Nelson's eyesight.

In 1801 at the Battle of Copenhagen, Nelson is reputed to have disregarded a direct order to disengage from Admiral Sir Hyde Parker. Legend has it that Nelson put his telescope to the eye-patch on his *blind eye* and claimed he couldn't see Parker's signal.

That's the short version of the story and gives us the phrase. The long version is more complex. Parker had huge faith in Nelson and arranged in advance that if he hoisted the disengage signal Nelson would have his blessing to ignore it, as he was the man in the thick of it and best placed to judge the next move. This he explained to his signals officer when he gave the order.

Nelson, however, had to do something to placate Colonel Stewart of the Royal Marines who was nearby when the order arrived. The colonel wasn't aware of the pre-arrangement and wouldn't have approved of such naval nonsense. Hence all the telescope drama.

The icing on this particular cake comes from the fact that Nelson wasn't *blind*. He did damage his eye at the Battle of Calvi in 1794 but he wasn't *blinded*, never wore an eye-patch, and never persuaded the navy to pay him disability compensation despite numerous attempts.

It is likely the expression had been used in English before Nelson but his fame brought common usage.

15. Running a Tight Ship

Running a tight ship is to be organised and efficient, and as you might guess it has nautical origins. *Tight* entered English as *tyght* around 1400 and it meant dense or compact but came from the Old Norse word *pettr* (watertight and close in texture) so the water connection was there from the start.

From the 1700s *tight* had come to also mean something which is drawn taut or stretched, like clothes whose fit is a little *tight* after a good dinner.

Both meanings are what give us a *tight ship* – the ship's hull is well caulked and *watertight* and her rigging lines are *tight* too – drawn taut and ready for use.

From 1830 you might find a person to be *tight* (drunk) in American English. *Sit tight* is from 1738. *Tight laced* arises in 1741 in both a figurative sense and if your corset was pulled too *tight*. *Tight lipped* is from 1872 and by 1871 you might wish someone to *sleep tight*. The idea of being *tight* with a close friend isn't as modern as you might expect, it dates back to 1956.

This chapter looks at how a captain might run a *tight ship* and what words shipboard discipline gave to the English language. Did you know the practice of *hazing* started on sailing ships?

Bootcamp

Bootcamps have a joint naval and military background which is miles away from fitness groups using the name today.

From the 1890s any naval or marine recruit was nicknamed a *Boot* for the leather leggings they wore. This arose during the Spanish-American War of 1898 and referred to the leg-wear of U.S. sailors. The camps where these new recruits were given basic training were hence called *bootcamps*.

By the 1920s the term had crossed the Atlantic and was used for any branch of the military in Britain but it remains specific to naval and marine camps in America.

Camps modelled on those ideas of physical work and discipline have opened since then to help troubled teens, instead of youth prisons, on both sides of the Atlantic.

Cat o' Nine Tails & No Room to Swing a Cat

The *cat of nine tails* was a short stick with nine knotted ropes, about half a yard (or metre) in length attached. It was used to flog seamen. Even one lash would take the skin off the man's back. Punishments of over a hundred lashes generally resulted in an agonising death.

The flogging usually took place on the main deck as the gun deck, with only four foot six inches (137m) of headroom you didn't have enough *room to swing a cat*, hence the phrase. Sometimes the prisoner would be forced to make the *cat* to be used on him, but later they were standard kit available from Royal Navy stores.

The *cat o' nine tails* largely replaced keelhauling (see below) and had a theoretical limit of 12 lashes, but certain captains ignored this restraint. It was abolished as a discipline method in 1879.

Hazing

The American tradition of *hazing* within student clubs, which has edged into general use as a term for the pranking or humiliation of a newcomer, has a surprising nautical origin.

In the 1800s, *hazing* was fairly common practice with captains subjecting their crews to unpleasant and unnecessary work in order to deprive them of sleep and maintain discipline through misery.

For example, in the classic sailing book "Two Years Before the Mast" Richard Henry Dana Jr. describes an entire crew being forced to stand watch needlessly on deck in the rain.

Keelhaul

Keelhauling was a cruel nautical punishment used both by pirates and the Royal Navy from the 1500s. The victim was dragged under the ship, while it was at sea, nearly drowning them, and typically ripping their bodies on barnacles, until they died or were near death. The prisoner would be dragged onto deck, allowed to recover their breath, and then the process was repeated. Sometimes one of the larger cannons was fired while the victim was underwater, hence causing pain in their ears and lead weights might be attached to their legs.

Keelhauling was replaced around 1700 by the milder, but still severe, punishment of whipping with a cat o' nine tails, see above.

Kissing the Gunner's Daughter

This phrase isn't common ashore but its unusual back story gives it a place here.

Discipline on board naval ships could be cruel and even the youngest members of the crew weren't exempt. Boys as young at twelve served and sometimes broke the rules. Some sailors believed if the boys weren't whipped on a Monday their ship would lack winds for the rest of the week.

Younger offenders, or those guilty of minor crimes, would be flogged on the gun deck while major offences were dealt with by the cat o' nine tails (see above) on the main deck. The boy would lean over a gun while being whipped, hence the idea of *kissing*, or hugging, *the gunner's daughter* i.e. the gun.

If the offence was greater the boy might be tied to the deck rings, which normally kept the gun fastened in place when not in use. This was called *marrying the gunner's daughter*, another reference to marriage as a form of *tying the kno*t or being *tied down* (see Getting Hitched in the Flying the Flag chapter).

Maroon

To be clear, here we're discussing the word for abandoning a person to their fate. The colour *maroon*, a very dark crimson, is named for the French word for chestnut, *marron*, and may even date back to Greek *maraon* for sweet chestnut.

Maroon in the nautical sense has shore links. A *maroon* was a fugitive negro slave living in the wild on Jamaica and other islands in the West Indies c. 1660s. The term came from *simarron* in French which was a corruption of *cimmaron* (wild, unruly, fugitive) in Spanish. By the 1690s to be *marooned* was to be lost in the wild, like those fugitives. By 1724 the idea of forcing someone to be lost in that way as a punishment had arisen.

The sailor would typically be abandoned on an uninhabited island. He was given a musket, some shot, a little gunpowder, and a bottle of water. The idea was that the prisoner could shoot themselves if rescue didn't come or they were dying of thirst.

The fictional pirate, Captain Jack Sparrow experienced *marooning* more than once in Disney's "Pirates of the Caribbean" film series, but managed to find rum to ease his pain. Not all victims were so lucky. Thankfully *marooning* was a very rare punishment.

Mutiny

Mutiny isn't an exclusively sea-based rebellion and the various *anti-mutiny* laws enacted apply equally to *mutinous* sailors, soldiers, and even aircrew. However the history of *mutiny* at sea is a long and varied one.

In 1520, three of Ferdinand Magellan's five ships on his circumnavigation of the world *mutinied* off the coast of Brazil, for example. Perhaps the best known *mutiny* is the one which took place on the *HMS Bounty* in 1789 when Christian Fletcher and his companions rose up against Captain Bligh.

Some of the mutineers returned to their last port, Tahiti, while others sailed on to the Pitcairn Islands.

Unbelievably Captain Bligh, who had sailed with Captain Cook earlier in his career, and the eighteen others set adrift in a small boat with minimal provisions managed the 4,000 mile journey to Timor where they caught a ship back to England.

Many of the *mutineers*, including Fletcher, were killed by the locals before they could be brought to justice (although their descendants survived on the islands). Bligh wasn't popular on his next posting either. Another *mutiny* against his authority took place when he was made governor of New South Wales in Australia. Clearly he had impressed his superiors, however, as he was promoted to Rear Admiral after his two year imprisonment there.

One alleged *mutineer*, midshipman Peter Hey who was on his first ever voyage, was captured on Tahiti and transported back to England, with a little pit stop for a shipwreck, to be tried. Convicted in 1792 he was sentenced to death but given a royal pardon and allowed to rejoin the Royal Navy where he had a successful career as captain and nearly made it to admiral before his death, aged 58.

Opinion is still divided on who the real villain was in the Bounty *mutiny*. Bligh had stopped rations, had men flogged, and clapped many of them in irons, while Fletcher had cast 19 men adrift to near certain death on the high seas.

Watch

In the traditional Royal Navy *watch* system a *watch* refers to a period of time and a group of crew-members. Crew whose work must continue throughout the day and night (managing sails, for example) are assigned to either starboard or port *watch*. Those groups may be subdivided into first port, second port, first starboard, second starboard etc. They are then assigned different hours of work. The opposite of these teams are the idlers (see the Crew chapter).

The word *watch* comes from Old English *waeccan* (keep *watch*, be awake) and *wakjan* in Proto-Germanic (be strong, be lively). The same linguistic concepts presumably inspired G.R.R. Martin's *Nightswatch* in "Game of Thrones".

16. Flying the Flag

Flags, for many centuries, were the main form of communication between ships and from sea to land. Banners served a similar purpose on land with armies but it was always easier to send a runner or a man on a horse to bring news of battle on land than it was to get a message to the admiral of a fleet.

As a result the names of flags and their uses at sea were many and various. Many flags have flapped their way into the dictionary. This chapter also includes a few knot and rope words.

Blue Flag

A sailing ship returning to port flew a *blue flag* or painted a blue band around its hull to indicate she had lost her captain, or other senior officer. Some sources believe this to be the root of *feeling blue* but that's unlikely because early references to *feeling blue*, or downcast, date to the 1400s, well before this practice.

The word *blue* entered English in the 1300s from Proto-Germanic roots. *Blue* wasn't even a colour in language in the time of Homer and his "Odyssey" where he describes the sea itself as being wine dark because the Greek language didn't have a word for the colour *blue* at that time.

Blue flags also indicate eco-friendly beaches and good water quality.

Blue Peter

The *blue peter* is the nickname given to the nautical signal flag for the letter P. The letter P in this case means all persons should report on board as the vessel is about to depart. The flag is royal blue with a white square in the centre and has been used since the 1800s.

The colours on nautical signal flags are chosen to be visible over long distances from ship to ship and ship to shore. They are red, blue, yellow, white, and black. One flag signals are chosen for either very urgent or very common signals. Other signals may be sent by combining flags. If a specific word needs to be spelled out, it can be done using the letter flags.

BBC has been broadcasting a beloved and long-running children's magazine style programme called *Blue Peter* since 1958. It was named after the maritime flag as it was intended to be a voyage of discovery for the viewers. The show's symbol is a sailing ship and the theme tune is a jaunty sea tune called Barnacle Bill.

Bunting

Bunting, a chain of tiny flags, or swags of draped fabric, is the perfect decoration for a celebration and it's another one we got from the sea.

To *bunt* is a nautical term for furling a sail in the middle. In the navy the sailor responsible for raising flags was called a *bunt*.

In a Flap

Hens had been doing it for centuries but it took the Royal Navy to give us the phrase *in a flap* for being in a state of worry or excitement.

With the advent of semaphore signalling (various positions of two handheld square flags signify different letters and messages can be sent and received at speed over line of sight) signallers would be observed signalling frantically, literally *in a flap*, when important events occurred.

After it entered land use the wonderful adjective *unflappable* arose in the 1950s, originally about Harold Macmillan the British Prime Minister, but we don't know if he ever did any semaphore signalling.

Flying Colours

The most common use of this phrase now is to say somebody passed a test *with flying colours*, but its origins lie with sea battles and flags.

The *colours* in question are the national flag of a ship. From the 1400s up to today, a warship will only lower her *colours* in the presence of a more senior ship, for example the admiral's ship. She'll only strike them completely if defeated in battle. A ship striking its colours is equivalent to a knight handing his sword over to the victor in a duel, tournament, or battle.

Hence if a warship emerges from a battle still *flying her own colours*, it means she has won.

Getting Hitched & Tying the Knot

Hitch isn't a particularly unusual word, but it is one with many meanings -

1. to move by jerks (she *hitched* up her skirts and ran)

2. to fasten by a knot/hook (the cowboy *hitched* his horse to the fence or connected a trailer to his tractor)

3. to get married

4. to *hitchhike*

It can also be a noun about difficulties - the wedding went off *without a hitch*, or can describe a period of military service.

Various traditions relating to knot tying link it to marriage and commitment ceremonies. We talk about a couple *tying the knot*, and in older traditions we have hand-fasting (where the couple's hands are literally tied together).

It's difficult to know if the marriage meaning of *hitch* pre-dated the knot meaning. *Hitch* comes from a middle English verb *hytchen* whose use dates back to the 14th century. Although *hitch* sounds like modern slang, it certainly isn't.

There's a key difference between a knot and a hitch (although not in the marital sense). A knot is used to tie two ropes together or a rope to itself, whereas a hitch joins the rope to another object such as a pole.

Jolly Roger

This pirate flag isn't linked to an actual pirate called Roger (although *King Roger* II of Sicily tried to claim it). The traditional flag of pirates was often decorated with a skull and crossbones but many different designs existed. Black Bart Roberts' *jolly roger* showed him sharing a glass of wine with the devil's skeleton.

Raising the *jolly roger* was an invitation to surrender, with the condition that anybody captured would be treated well (see walk the plank in the Scurvy Pirates chapter).

Unfortunately the origins of this flag are confused at best. Experts disagree on when it entered English with dates ranging from the 11th to the 18th century. Stealing on the high-seas is an old tradition so I'd lean towards the earlier dates.

The best explanation I can find for its origin comes from British naval history. In 1694 the British Admiralty commanded English privateers (state-approved pirates) to fly a plain red flag to identify themselves. This makes sense as otherwise they might be mistaken for mere thieves, or the Royal Navy itself. Thereafter the term "*red jacking*" came to mean piracy.

However the plain red flag already had a meaning well-known to sailors - danger. In particular, the red flag signalled an explosive cargo aboard. The red flag meaning "this ship's captain will not give quarter" became known as *La Jolie Rouge* (the pretty red in French).

Privateers chose a plain black flag instead. If you were attacked by a ship flying such a flag you knew to give up or face death. Over time the privateer captains embellished their flags. Each pirate captain ended up with a unique version of the *jolly roger*. They added skeletons, skulls, and cutlasses but few favoured the legendary skull and crossbones design.

It probably helped the intimidatory nature of the flag that in English slang *Roger* was an alternative name for the devil.

Knot

Tying *knots* is a vital skill for any sailor and the word has various uses afloat. Rigging a sailing ship requires various *knots*, but *knots* are also associated with speed.

The *knot* has been the nautical measure of speed since the 1630s thanks to a simple device. A log would be thrown overboard while the ship was under sail, attached to it was a line with *knots* tied at regular distances (1/120 of a mile between each *knot* was standard). The ship's speed was then measured by an hourglass for a set time (a half minute for example). The number of *knots* payed out on the line, was the speed.

One *knot* became equivalent to one nautical mile. Ten knots at sea is roughly equal to 11.5 miles per hour on land. The use of the log also gave us the concepts of a logbook and logging in (see log in the Parts of a Ship chapter).

Knots themselves existed on land before they were used at sea but sailors invented new ones for specific tasks such as mooring boats, and quick release *knots* for loosening sails.

Knot is a word the Vikings gave us. English acquired *knot* from *knutr* in Old Norse via German *Knoten*, Dutch *knot*, and finally as *cnotta* in Old English.

One final *knot* story is a sailor's yarn that one day a witch was persuaded by a sailor to sell him some wind. Like Odysseus and the bag of wind from the Greek god of winds Aeolos, the sailor was presented with a piece of rope with three *knots* in it. She warned him to untie the first for a breeze, the second for a steady wind, and the third only as a last resort.

The sailor went to sea, delighted with his gift. He untied the first and a gentle breeze billowed out his sails. His ship moved, but too slowly for his liking so he loosened the second knot and sped away from shore for his destination. After transacting his business there he boarded his ship once more and looked at the final knot. It was getting dark and he wanted to return home quickly.

He untied the final *knot* and unleashed a hurricane that split the sails of his ship and sank it below the angry waves.

Know the Ropes

Knowing the ropes (1840s) on a sailing ship was vital. Sailors had to learn the rigging of each new vessel on which they served and how to tie all the appropriate *knots*. This led to *knowing the ropes, show him the ropes*, and *learning the ropes* being expressions for job training.

Rope entered Old English spelled as *rap* from a Proto-Germanic root.

There could be up to ten miles (16km) of *ropes* in the rigging of the larger ships and the *ropes* had hundreds of different functions and names yet most of the *ropes* were the same colour and size so a new crew member had to learn their use from their position.

Nail Colours to the Mast

Since the 1800s if you *nail your colours to the mast* you're taking a stand. You won't be talked around. You are determined.

The meaning is the same afloat, although more extreme.

The *colours* in question are the national flag of a warship and they would only be lowered in the case of defeat. Ships whose crew was determined not to surrender would make a show of sending a crew member aloft with a hammer and nails to fix their *colours* firmly to the mast in advance of engagement. *Nailing the colours* sent a clear signal to watching ships that they would fight to the death.

Red Flag / Bloody Flag

A *red flag* raised by pirates meant that no quarter would be given, no prisoners would be taken. The *red flag* meaning "this ship's captain will not give quarter" became known over time as *La Jolie Rouge* (the pretty red in French).

Sail Under False Colours

In the 1500 and 1600s the only way to identify a ship, particularly from a distance at sea, was its *colours* (its national flag). Most nations had distinct forms of rigging or styles of ships but ships were often captured during battles and then used in the captor's navy so you might easily have a Portuguese ship in the British navy attacking a French ship.

The identifying flags, or *colours*, were vital. You didn't want to fire on a friendly ship. Some captains kept a selection of such national flags (captured during battles or bought ashore) to fly as a disguise, enabling their ship to sneak close to their prey. Only at the last moment would the correct *colours* be run up the mast.

The phrase is now used to indicate any subterfuge or deceit.

Splice

Splice has been in English since 1520 and was originally a sailor's word. It came to English from Middle Dutch *splissen* (to *splice*) which was borrowed from French *épisser* (same meaning) but has origins in the Proto-Germanic verb *splei* – to *split*, especially for describing how shards split away from flint.

Splice is used on board ships to describe the process of joining the strands of two ropes but its use is widespread ashore too. From the 1830s *splice* became an informal term for getting married. From 1912 *splicing* referred to joining celluloid in the film industry. In 1975 it became a method of joining strands of DNA in genetics labs.

Take Down a Peg or Two

This idea of deflating somebody's ego comes from warship flags and dates to the 1500s.

A warship flew her identifying flags at a specific height dictated by a series of *pegs* in the base of the mast around which the flag ropes were run. If you wanted to lower the flag slightly, as a gesture of deference to the arrival of a more senior ship, for example the admiral's ship, you would move a *peg* down a slot, thus lowering your own flag.

Union Jack

The distinctive red, white, and blue flag of Great Britain is called the *Union Jack* and has strong maritime links. The flag was created by joining the English Saint George's flag (red cross on white) with the Scottish Saint Andrew's flag (white saltire on blue).

After countless wars and the beheading of Mary Queen of Scots by her cousin Queen Elizabeth, Mary's son James became King James I of England and King James VI of Scotland in 1603, thus taking an important step towards the formation of the United Kingdom.

Three years later this was celebrated with a new flag called the *Flag of Britain*. By 1625 it was called the *Flag of the Union*. Over time this became known as *Jack's Flag* or the *Union Jack*. The *Jack* in question being the nickname for James.

The *Jack* link to James is compelling but it should be noted that any flag, especially one flown at the bow of a ship, to indicate her nationality is called a *Jack*. So a

Union Jack is literally the *jack flag* of the United Kingdom.

Purists claim the flag is called the *Grand Union* when flown ashore and should only be called the *Union Jack* when flown on a ship. Technically only the monarch's vessel can fly the *Union Jack* while sailing but others can fly it in port.

Others claim the flag can be flown upside down (yes there is a right way up on that distinctive X-shaped design) to signal distress. Flying it upside down would be noticed by another British ship and might not be noticed by crews from other nations so could be used as a subtle plea for help.

Wales, in case you were wondering, was already joined to England before King James arrived, but the formal creation of the United Kingdom of Great Britain was in 1707.

Vexillology

This one isn't in common use but it's the perfect word for a chapter about flags. *Vexillology* is the scientific study of flags including their history, symbolism and usage. So if you love the idea of semaphore, maritime and lighthouse service communication flags, and country flags, you're a *vexillologist*. There's even an International Federation of *Vexillological* Associations.

The word is a relatively recent one, first used around 1959 and comes from *vexillum* (Latin for flag) and *logia* (Greek suffix for study).

Yellow Flag

A *yellow flag* is flown to indicate the presence of illness, often yellow fever, on board. This flag was sometimes flown to avoid confrontation or boarding by pirates.

17. Maritime Fashion

A naval officer in dress uniform will always turn heads and as discussed in the Eponym chapter we have the sea to thank for items like *blazers, bikinis,* and *bermuda shorts.*

The Victorian trend for dressing small children in sailor suits has mostly passed, thank goodness, but did you know the wide-legged flares of the 1970s came from the sea too? *Bell-bottomed trousers* were ex-naval issue trousers bought cheaply, dyed into vibrant shades, and sold to start a massive London fashion that spread worldwide.

Several items of clothing which started life on the waves have entered the English dictionary and here's a selection.

Breeches Buoy

A *breeches buoy* is a lifebuoy with a leg harness or canvas *breeches* (short trousers) attached which is used to transfer a person between ships, from a boat to shore where there's no landing spot, or from a wrecked vessel. They were used extensively to land lighthouse keepers onto rock stations and in lifeboat rescues. It's not elegant and there's a high chance of a dunking, but they have saved many lives when a more traditional transfer wasn't possible.

Buoy's word origin is explained in the I Do Like To Be Beside the Seaside chapter.

Breeches entered English in the 1100s as Old English *brec* to describe a garment worn by men, covering the body and waist to the knees. The word reached English via Norse, Dutch, and German with a meaning linked to broken or forked to indicate the two legs of the *breeches*. Trouser-like leg coverings weren't popular in Roman or Greek civilisations (except in their colder outposts) but were known in Gaul (modern day France) and the orient at that time.

Trousers only became known as pants in American English from the 1840s onwards.

Breech as it relates to *breech births* and the *breech* of a gun all come from the idea of *breeches* covering the rear or hindquarters.

Castoffs

Cast off clothes were originally the clothes worn by sailors on shore which he wouldn't need on ship as they wouldn't handle the rough work or had long elements which might be caught in rigging. Similarly some mooring ropes would be left behind on the dock and they were also called *cast offs*. This led to the idea of *cast offs* being finished with and less valued.

The terms *casting on* (starting) and *casting off* (finishing) in knitting may relate to this idea as stitches *cast off* are no longer required or used.

Lanyard

A *lanyard* is a cord worn by sailors to secure items they need during their work. In the Royal Navy, for example, their knife was attached to the *lanyard* at the front of the seaman's body at a length that allowed him to reach it one-handed while in the rigging. The *lanyard* was worn around their neck but under the collar of their jacket or shirt to prevent strangulation issues.

Pirates wore *lanyards* for their daggers and pistols and today's Sea Scouts often have a *lanyard* as part of their uniform. Modern usage is most likely to be a *lanyard* to hang identification badges or security swipe-cards.

Lanyard entered English via Middle English as *lainer* in the late 1300s as "thong for fastening clothing or armour) from Old French *laniere* (leather thong) with relationships to similar words in German and Old Saxon.

Rigout

To be well *rigged out* or in *a nice rigout* means that you're smartly dressed. The expression comes from sailing ships.

The *rig* of a ship is her masts, spars, rigging, and sails. A sailing ship who was *well rigged out* had a neat, functional appearance that was pleasing to the eye. A *rigout* of clothing is much the same.

Sloppy

Sloppy is used now to describe something as messy, ill fitting, or slovenly. It gained that meaning from the Royal Navy.

Sloppe as a word to describe a loose fitting garment was used by Chaucer so its roots are old. The navy didn't have a formal uniform for many years. In 1632, because of the tattered clothes worn by its sailors, the navy ordered each ship to carry *a slops chest* filled with basic clothes to be issued as needed. They rarely fit the wearer and often were old or musty. Sometimes the cost of such *slops* were deducted from pay. The practice led to the notion of a *sloppy dresser* (the opposite of a snappy dresser) and hence to *sloppy* in the more general sense used today.

A *sloppy joe* in the 1940s was a loose fitting sweater worn by females, but by the 1960s described a popular American loose hamburger dish.

Tattoo

A *tattoo* as a decoration inked into the skin (as opposed to a *military tattoo* – a signal to call soldiers, and sailors, to quarters at night) was first used in English by a rather famous mariner, Captain Cook, in 1769. He recorded it from a Polynesian word (from Tahiti or Samoa) *tatau* which described a puncture on the skin. Cook recorded one of his crew had acquired a *tatau* on their body.

By 1902 the Century Dictionary was listing them as common on "sailors and uncivilised people".

However such marks were known in English before the 1700s under a different name. A traveller might carry a Jerusalem Cross (from 1690s) to record their pilgrimage to the Holy Land.

Many Roman Catholic sailors chose to have a crucifix *tattoo* so they could receive an appropriate burial if they were lost at sea without other identification. Another popular design was a pig on the foot or near the kneecap. There are many superstitions surrounding pigs held by seafarers.

18. Nautical Phrases

Nautical phrases are so colourful it's not surprising they've ruled the waves and the land for centuries. Many are so ingrained in English now that we forget their watery origins. *Bitter end, booby trap, clean bill of health, flaking out, hand over fist, slush fund,* and *high profile* all came to us from the sea.

As mentioned before there is a tendency to ascribe nautical origins to words without any proof and this was particularly true when I researched phrases for this book. If your favourite sea saying isn't here, there's a pretty good chance it sounds like something a sailor would say but actually has land-based origins. Examples of these include – *armed to the teeth* (knights, not pirates), *creaking at the seams* (corsets not boats), *rock the boat* (politicians not sailors), and *long shot* (archery rather than ship's cannons).

Above Board

If a pirate ship approached a merchant ship the majority of the attackers hid below decks to avoid frightening their prey. This was vital as pirate ships typically carried many more crew-members so they'd have a numerical advantage in any hand-to-hand combat. Hence if the crew was *above board*, all was well.

Equally if cargo was stored in plain view on the deck of a ship it was unlikely to be avoiding the excisemen. If it was hidden below the boards of the deck, it might be illegally smuggled cargo.

The maritime origins of this phrase are open to dispute, however. Some experts believe those being *above board* were card-players not hiding their cards beneath the table in order to cheat. It should perhaps be noted that sailors enjoyed gaming on board ship and on dry land so the phrase may have travelled in either direction.

All Hands on Deck

This was one of the bo'sun's calls (see bo'sun in the Crew Chapter). Crew were usually divided into two or three watches. One watch team was working while the others were eating or sleeping. If the call for *All Hands on Deck* was issued, the entire crew was required either for orders to be given, to sail in dangerous conditions, or perhaps for a battle.

The phrase is used ashore now whenever all members of a team are needed to pitch in, often when time is short or pressure is high.

Anchors Aweigh / Away

The correct spelling is *anchors aweigh* but as it relates to readying for departure (at sea or on land) you can see where the *anchors away* variant came from.

First used in print in the 1600s the expression is actually about the *weight* on an *anchor*. An *anchor* which is *aweigh* is one which is putting pressure on the rope or cable being used to pull it up. The sailors hauling away haven't finished bringing the *anchor* up, but it's on its way.

The addition of an "a-" prefix to words is a popular one amongst the sailing community. Other examples include *afloat, ashore, aboard, adrift*, and *aground*.

Anchors Aweigh is a song written by Charles A. Zimmerman in 1906 with lyrics by Alfred Hart Miles and it was adopted as the official song of the United States Navy.

Anchors Aweigh, the movie starring Frank Sinatra and Gene Kelly, was a popular musical comedy hit in 1945.

Between the Devil and the Deep Blue Sea

This expression entered English in the 1600s and is about being stuck between two tough, unpalatable choices. A choice between the devil himself or drowning in *the deep blue sea* would be a poor choice indeed.

Greek mythology gives us a clue to its origins. In Homer's "Odyssey" poor Odysseus, on his protracted journey home from the Siege of Troy, is caught between Scylla (a six-headed monster, or devil) and Charybdis (a sea whirlpool).

Another version claims it's all about ship maintenance. The *devil* is the seam between the deck planking and the topmost plank of the side of the ship. This seam must be watertight and when it needed filling (caulking) a sailor had to be suspended *between the devil and the deep blue sea* to do the work in a very precarious position.

The Bitter End / The End of One's Rope

The anchor is vital on a ship. The anchor rope on old sailing ships was secured to a wooden post on the ship called the *bitt*. As the anchor rope was paid out and the anchor sank to the sea floor the last section of rope to unwind from the *bitt* was *the bitter end* and when you reached that point there was no more rope to use, the anchor had gone as far as it could.

Letting out the anchor in this way was hard physical work, by the end of it you were *at the end of one's rope*. This was particularly true if the anchor had failed to catch on the seabed because you were literally *in deep water* and unable to secure your boat.

The *bitter end* was in nautical use from 1627 and came ashore in English around 1835.

Booby Prize / Booby Trap

A *booby* is a red or blue footed sea bird which totters around rather gormlessly. You'll find videos online, they're worth viewing. Their meat wasn't particularly tasty for sailors, but was eaten if nothing else was available. Darwin studied them during his voyage on *The Beagle*.

Booby comes from the Spanish term *bobo*, meaning foolish or slow-witted because the birds were easy to catch and unafraid of men. *Booby* entered English in the 1590s to describe a stupid person, thanks to the seabirds.

By the 1880s the idea of a *booby prize* for loser in a contest had been invented. Around the same time a schoolboy prank at the expense of those less intelligent was coined as a *booby trap*. The more lethal idea of a military *booby trap* didn't arise until World War I.

Brought up Short

To be brought up *short* is to be suddenly halted, perhaps by an unanticipated change in events.

Unlike motorcars with emergency brakes, sailing ships take time to stop. This was a problem in maritime battles but the solution was simple, drop the anchors. The vessel would shudder to a noisy halt. This process was called being *brought up short*.

Burn Your Boats

Burning your boats is a synonym of the military phrase *burn your bridges*. Both mean to cut off all retreat and hence fully commit to forward action.

Legend has it that Greek and Roman armies would indicate their intention to stay in an invaded area by *burning the boats* they had used to reach the place, thus encouraging their soldiers to survive and thrive in the new land. There would be no retreat or mutiny.

The phrase entered English in reference to Hernando Cortes' landing at Vera Cruz in Mexico in 1519 when another legend has it he took the same incendiary approach.

However history tells us he wasn't so foolish. Instead he ran eight of his eleven ships aground and ordered the other three to sail out of sight. He wanted his troops to think there was no retreat, but was sensible enough not to actually *burn his boats*, which would be needed for the return trip at some point. Hernando was a very successful conquistador who caused the fall of the Aztec Empire and brought most of Mexico under Spanish rule.

By and Large
{with thanks to Peter Sheehan}

This phrase doesn't sound particularly maritime in nature but bear with me.

When a wind is blowing from a behind a ship's direction of travel it is said to be *large*. This use dates back to the 1500s at least. The favourable wind allows *large* sails to be set and the captain may sail as he wishes.

The *by* part is trickier to explain. To have a sailing ship *by the wind* is to face into the wind or within six compass points of its direction. This is much harder than sailing with the *wind at your back*.

To sail *by and large* means the ship had to be able to sail both with a favourable wind (which square-rigged ships could do) and also to sail against the wind. It may seem counter-intuitive that a sail ship could make headway against the wind, but it is possible, by using triangular sails to get sideways force much like airplane wings, combined with clever use of the rudder.

Sailing ships which combined both square and triangular sails in their rigging, such as the famous 1800s windjammer *The Cutty Sark,* were able to sail *by and large* even in contrary wind conditions.

Chock-a-block
{with thanks to Peter Sheehan}

The idea of something being so full that it is *chock-a-block* comes from tackle *blocks* in the rigging. If two such *blocks* are so close to each other there can be no movement in the sails. The phrase dates to the 1800s.

Additionally the word *chock* means to secure items tightly on deck to prevent damage if the seas are rough, perhaps by using wooden wedges, or *chocks*, to stop movement. The opposite of that is the aviation cry of *chocks away* when wedges were removed from the wheels of aircraft to allow them to taxi onto the runway.

Chock is likely to be related to the idea of *choking* something and dates back to 1400s in English.

Chock-a-block is also sometimes phrased as *being chockers*.

Clean Bill of Health

If your finances are given a *clean bill of health* you probably have cash stashed away for a rainy day and plenty to pay your daily expenses, but the expression has, as you might expect, a strong link to *healthy* bodies rather than other affairs, and in particular *healthy* sailors.

The port authority issued a *clean bill of health* certificate to any ship entering their port once they confirmed no sailor on board had a contagious disease and that no such problem had been in their port of departure either. If this wasn't the case a *foul bill of health* would be issued and the ship might be put in quarantine (see the Salmagundi chapter).

Cold Enough to Freeze the Balls off a Brass Monkey {with thanks to Brendan Tierney}

This expression is commonly believed to have originated in the Royal Navy because they stacked iron cannon balls on a *brass* tray. Thanks to metals freezing at different temperatures the balls would roll off the tray in cold weather. Unfortunately, despite being an evocative, and slightly ribald, story - this is utter rubbish.

The *balls* weren't stacked in pyramids on ships because the rolling of the vessel would cause them to roll off and potentially injure the crew. From 1769 they were placed on planks, called *shot garlands* (not *monkeys*) with holes cut out to hold them in place. Plus, the relative expansion differences in brass versus iron mean a temperature drop of 100 degrees celsius is required to cause even one millimetre of a problem – in which case the ship would have frozen to smithereens long before the *balls* rolled.

The boys who carried the gun powder were called *powder monkeys* so there may be some link there but it hasn't been proven and interestingly for a phrase supposed to have originated in the Age of Sail, the first use in print was 1978. Some more polite versions of the phrase (nose, tail etc) were in use during the 1800s, but none go back far enough in time to link it to a verifiable nautical origin.

Cut and Run

Sailing ships were sometimes required to make a swift getaway from an anchorage. To achieve this, one crew-member would *cut* the anchor rope while others would *cut* the smaller ties binding up furled sails. The phrase to describe this, *cut and run*, entered English around 1590 but didn't apply to land-based escapes until the 1800s.

This practise, while costly in anchors, was effective and considerably swifter than laboriously raising the anchor and untying various knots. The process also gave us phrases such as *cut loose*, *cut the ties that bind*, and even *break out* as loose sails after this process are said to have *broken out*.

Cut to the Chase

The *chase* in this case is that of one ship pursuing another, either for naval glory or simply to steal cargo. Getting a sailing ship underway from a stationary position, or increasing her speed from a steady pace, isn't a swift process so if the *chaser* spotted a chance *shortcuts* could be taken, literally, by *cutting* the anchor rope and *cutting* any ties holding sails in a furled position, thus allowing a rapid burst of speed in pursuit of their quarry.

This origin for the phrase is disputed by movie fans who argue that directors would order editors to *cut to the chase* in order to increase the pace of their films.

As a nautical film buff I'm including both, you can make your own decision.

Dead in the Water

A ship which is *dead in the water* is without wind or engine power, immobile and vulnerable to attack. This phrase is now used to describe other such powerless states of anything or anybody unable to operate effectively, such as "the economy is *dead in the water*" or "the exposed corrupt politician's campaign was *dead in the water*".

Dead Man's Chest

This phrase has fictional nautical roots. Robert Louis Stevenson wrote a pirate ditty for his famous novel "Treasure Island" which included the phrase.

Fifteen men on the dead men's chest
Yo-ho-ho, and a bottle of rum!
Drink and the devil had done for the rest
Yo-ho-ho, and a bottle of rum!

Stevenson never offered an explanation of the rhyme, but its meaning was uncovered recently thanks to research published by the Royal Geographical Society.

In the early 1700s Edward Teach (the pirate Blackbeard) marooned thirty of his crew on a tiny rocky island off Tortola in the British Virgin Islands which was known to sailors as *The Dead Man's Chest* because it was inhospitable to life other than insects and lizards and had no fresh water source.

Each mutinous sailor was given a bottle of rum and a cutlass in the hope they'd kill each other but when Teach returned a month later 15 men had survived. It's not recorded what action he took next. The island is now called Dead Chest Island.

Deadwood

Deadwood in ship-building (from the 1700s) are heavy longitudinal timbers at either end of the keel to which are attached to the bow and stern. The term is now used to describe people who simply along for the ride, wasting space, and are dragging everybody else down. It's also a way to describe bowling pins (1858) which have fallen but now block those still standing.

Devil to Pay and No Pitch Hot

You may be more familiar with *the devil to pay*. It arose from the idea of a pact with the *devil* like the one

Faustus made. Its use pre-dates the more nautical and entirely separate *devil to pay*.

The *devil* on the ship doesn't have horns or cloven hooves, it is the seam between planking on the hull of a wooden ship and *paying it* meant sealing it with old ropes and hot tar. Doing so without *hot pitch* would be impossible which is what *devil to pay and no pitch hot* means. The sailors were expressing impatience that they were ready to work, but couldn't without *hot pitch*.

The same maintenance task is referenced in the expression *between the devil and the deep blue sea* (see above). Clearly caulking the *devil* seam (the longest on the ship) was a tricky, dangerous, and yet important task to keep the ship afloat.

Dressing Down

One potential source for *dressing down* - an unpleasant ticking off from your superiors - is sail maintenance. The canvas sails common in the Age of Sail become waterlogged easily and would then be harder to handle and prone to damage. As a result they had to be treated with oils and other preservatives while they were fully rigged and open rather than furled up.

To *dress down* both sides of a sail, while hanging from ropes, with the wet canvas slapping you in the face was an unpleasant, but necessary task, which led to the expression – to receive *a dressing down*.

Enough to Make a Sailor a Pair of Pants
{with thanks to Nell Jenda}

Upon seeing a small patch of blue sky on a grey day this expression asks the vital question *is it enough to make a sailor a pair of pants* (or trousers in the U.K., where pants are an undergarment)? Literally you're asking if the blue sky will expand to improve the day or will be it be swamped by the surrounding grey?

Traditionally a sailor's uniform would include a pair of blue *trouser pants* and in the case of the British Royal Navy they were large bell-bottomed affairs so the size of fabric used was significant. There's an alternative version *enough to make a Dutchman a pair of trousers* which again has an implied emphasis on volume of fabric as the Dutch national costume includes huge baggy blue trousers.

Faffing

Faffing, or *faffing about*, is more used in British and Australian English than in America but wherever it is deployed it describes ineffectual dithering activity.

Faff has been used since the 1800s and may be descended from *faffle* from the 1500s which had the same meaning but also described something idly flapping in the wind.

This second meaning gives us the nautical clue. A wind which blew inconsistently, and hence was completely useless to a ship and her crew, was *faffing about.*

First Rate

To say something is *first rate* is to say it's of top quality. *First rate* was first applied to warships thanks to Samuel Pepys (1633-1703) the famous diarist who witnessed the restoration of King Charles II and the Great Fire of London.

Pepys became the First Secretary to the Admiralty and created the *first, second, and third rate* classifications of warships in 1677. *First rate* ships carried 100 guns and 800 men, *second rate* had 82 guns and 530 men, while *third rate* ships only carried 74 guns and 460 men. The ratings continued down to *sixth rate*.

A *first rate* ship of the line (line meaning battle line, the first row of ships into battle) in the 1750s was probably the finest ship of the Age of Sail. She was the flagship of any group she sailed with and always carried the admiral or most senior officers. She cost about £95 million sterling to build in today's money and was a rarity in any navy. During the 1700s the Royal Navy had about five or six such ships at any one time. Each served about 70 years, undergoing many re-fittings. *The Victory,* for example, was forty years old when she saw action at the Battle of Trafalgar and had been rebuilt, twice.

By the 1680s the phrase *first rate* had passed from naval into general use.

Interestingly a similar phrase about categorisation by quality – *first water* – isn't remotely nautical but comes from the diamond trade.

Fish Stinks from the Head Down
{with thanks to Rita Fitzsimons}

A fish stinks (or rots) from the head down means that if a country or an organisation fails or is corrupt, that problem started at the top.

It's an ancient proverb claimed by countries as diverse as China, Russia, Poland, Greece, and England, but it may have originated in Turkey as it was recorded in 1768 by

James Porter, the British ambassador to the Ottoman Empire at the time.

Even in Turkey the phrase was metaphorical from the outset as residents of sea port Constantinople would have been well aware that a *fish rots* from its guts first, not its head. It perhaps speaks to the universality of corruption in leadership that so many countries took the phrase to heart.

Flaking Out

One chain you never want to break in a ship is the anchor chain so it was regularly laid out on the deck to have its links checked. This process was called *flaking out*. As a result lying on the deck in the sunshine became known as *flaking out*.

This should not be confused with being *a flake* or *flaky* from the 1920s which were ways to describe somebody addicted to cocaine and hence unreliable.

Get a Word in Edgeways

It can be tricky to sneak into a conversation which is so fast flowing that putting forward your own thoughts can seem impossible. This is where the skill of *getting a word in edgeways* (or *edgewise*) is handy.

The expression was coined ashore in Britain but found its inspiration in the sailing skills of the 1600s. *Edging forward* (this time at sea, rather than in conversation) was a useful sailing skill for making slow advances at sea using small tacking movements against a headwind. By the end of the 1600s the idea of *edging* in speech had been recorded but *getting a word in edgeways* took off from the 1800s and is still in use today.

Go by the Board

If something goes *by the board* it is finished with, no longer of any use.

The *board* in question is the plank of the side of a wooden ship and the idea originated in the 1700s with descriptions of broken masts going *by the board* – hanging over the side, no use to anybody and possibly dangerous to the vessel. A mast in that condition would typically be cut loose. The idea on land is the same – something past its usefulness, ready to be abandoned.

Gungho

Gung ho means eager or overzealous enthusiasm.

Gung ho entered English during World War II. General Evans Carlson of the U.S. marines was impressed with the name and work ethic of the Chinese industrial co-operatives which had been co-founded by a New Zealander friend of his - *kung hou* - which translates as "work together in harmony".

He explained the idea to his soldiers - a group of workers all dedicated to a single objective. He held *gung ho* meetings to explain orders and overcome issues without regard for traditional hierarchies. The phrase caught on and later spread throughout the marines and entered general parlance.

Gung ho gained a high profile when it was used as the title of a 1943 box-office hit film starring Randolph Scott about Carlson's battalion's innovative commando-style attack on Makin Island in the Pacific Ocean in 1942.

Hand over Fist

To do something *hand over fist* is to do so swiftly and without stopping. A particularly alluring example is to make money *hand over fist*.

The idea comes from hauling on a rope where the sailor grabs a rope, makes a *fist* around it and then reaches out with their other *hand* to pull along the rope. The original idea, probably starting in the 1700s, was of making steady progress but over time the speed has increased and now the expression implies the sailor is making very fast work of that hauling.

Hard and Fast

To hold to a belief without doubt is to hold it *hard and fast* and it comes from 1800s seafaring lingo. A ship which is firmly beached on the land is said to be *hard and fast*.

The term *hard* describes a firm beach or slope, ideal for hauling boats out of the water and *to make fast* is another way of saying to tie up firmly. The combination of both describes a well-secured ship on the shore.

High and Dry
{with thanks to Peter Sheehan}

If you're *high and dry* you're stranded without hope of escape or recovery.

If a boat is *high and dry* then it is (pardon the pun) in the same boat. This phrase originally described ships which had been beached above the *high* water line and had dried out, i.e. had been out of the water for some time with little prospect of being floated again.

Early uses of this phrase occurred in 1783.

High Profile

High profile (and indeed the corresponding *low profile*) terms are used widely today but they were originally secret marine terms.

During the Cold War (1945-1990) the East and West kept a close eye on each others' movements on land and sea. In naval terms they categorised shipping using the terms *high* and *low profile*.

High profile covered anything from battleships up to aircraft carriers while *low profile* included innocent fishing trawlers and surfaced submarines.

The terms crept into general English via journalism.

Profile as a word comes from Italian into English in the 1650s as a drawing or outline of anything from *profilo* and *profilare* (to draw out).

High Seas

The concept of sailing the *high seas* does prompt the question – are there *low seas*? Sadly the answer is no.

The *high seas* are a legal definition. They are the waters beyond the territorial waters (usually a 12 mile limit, but not exclusively – for example Ireland's territorial waters encompass space ten times the amount of her landmass) of any country. Essentially the *high seas* are waters unclaimed by any country. Roughly 50% of the seas on planet Earth are *high seas*.

This sounds wonderful, a free place in the world, a wild frontier. The reality is the opposite. The *high seas* are most at risk of environmental pollution, species extinction, and other issues. There are few protected habitats in the *high seas*.

The original limit for territorial waters was the three mile limit. It was set in 1702 and the range was three miles because that was the range of firing by cannons in land-based batteries. The move in the U.S.A. to the more common twelve mile limit came about in 1988.

In the Offing

If something is likely to happen soon it's *in the offing*, for example "Bob's boss says there's a promotion *in the offing*."

The area of the sea which can be seen from the shore is called *the offing*. So if you spotted a ship in *the offing* it would be arriving in harbour soon. For example, cargo ships will anchor *in the offing* at the entrance to port, waiting for the right tidal conditions to enter and dock, or waiting for a berth to become available.

The phrase *in the offing* dates back to at least the 1600s about ships but the figurative phrase didn't arise until 1850s America.

Jump Ship

To *jump ship* is to abandon your post, before your time is served. The idea came about with sailors literally *jumping* over the side and swimming to freedom when their ship was close to land. This wasn't surprising in the days of the Shanghai Press or pressgang when sailors, or even landlubbers, were forced to serve on ships.

Jump entered English in the 1520s from either the Swedish word *gumpa* (spring or *jump*) or from *jumba* or *yumpa* (to rock) dialect words in the south west of France which might have snuck into English during the Hundred Years War between Britain and France.

Kettle of Fish

A *kettle* is a metal container used to heat water over a flame, or in the modern versions using an electric element inside the *kettle* itself. It's vital equipment for making tea. There's also a *fish kettle*, a long oblong saucepan with lid, used for cooking an entire fish. They were once found in most kitchens.

Kettle entered English as *cetil* in Old English and is also found in Mercian (*citel*), Saxon (*ketel*), Frisian (*zetel*), Dutch and German. It probably springs from the Latin word *catillus* – a deep pan or dish for cooking. The change to spelling with a k rather than a c may be an influence from the Old Norse word *ketill* (*kettle*).

These *kettles* all appeared long before tea reached Britain (in the 1660s thanks to King Charles II) and the *kettle* in *kettle of fish* is unlikely to be a *tea-kettle* (first used in print c. 1769).

Kettle of fish is first mentioned in the early 1700s as a complex and bungled affair and some believe this comes from the Scottish culinary tradition of cooking several fish in a *kettle* on outdoor trips, leading to a rather messy collection of fish, bones, and skin in the *kettle*.

Other links between *kettles* and fish are either geological – a *kettle* is a deep circular hollow in a riverbed thanks to erosion, or fishing – a *kittle* (mentioned in the Magna Charta in Anglo-Latin as *kidellus*, c. 1200) which was a net, or series of nets set in river mouths to catch fish in a weir-like system.

All three forms of *kettle* would lead to a random collection of fish all jumbled up together and this is what gives us the phrase.

Knock Off

Galley ships used to be rowed to the rhythm of a hammer hitting a wooden block. When the mallet ceased striking, the galley slaves could rest. This led to the idea of people *knocking off* work.

Loose Cannon

From the 1600s to the 1800s warships' primary weapons were *cannon*. When fired they had a huge recoil so they were mounted on wheeled gun carriages and secured with ropes when not in use. A *loose cannon* was one which had broken frees of its restraints. Rolling around the gun deck it would be liable to cause damage and injuries.

There's little evidence *loose cannon* was used by sailors themselves but Victor Hugo, inspired by the concept, included it in his 1874 novel "Ninety Three" describing a chaotic scene on a ship when a *cannon* came *loose*. This scene was referenced in an English novel in 1875 in a more metaphorical sense and the phrase crept into common use to describe an unorthodox person who damages an organisation with their wild actions.

Loose End

Loose ends are the bane of fictional detectives. Every little clue must be chased down. Being at a *loose end* is different, but related. Being at a *loose end* implies enforced idleness and on board a ship a good captain abhorred having his crew at *loose ends*.

Maintenance of the ropes on a ship is an endless task so if the captain spotted a crew-member without productive work he would order them to check the ropes and bind *loose ends*.

The idea of *tying up loose ends*, in use since the 1800s, came from sailors making final checks to ropes before casting off for a voyage, although now it's more likely to be an urge to finalise small details before submitting work for inspection, or announcing whodunnit.

Making a Pass

Making a pass at a person, a ship, or in swordplay should all be entirely different events but there's always a fear that making the first move romantically could cause trouble if either party is reading the signals wrong. This is true with this phrase in all three modes of use.

To *make a pass* in swordplay is to make a lunge or thrust and it's used with this meaning in "Hamlet" in 1604.

During the Age of Sail *making a pass* wasn't between two combatants but between warships. The ships would make a side by side *pass* of each other to enable the captains to assess gun-power. This would sometimes involve firing at the same time because the guns were primarily mounted in the sides of the ships. To fire a broadside, the ships had to be roughly parallel.

Sailors may have brought the term ashore to their notorious romantic lives when the mutual "checking out" was a precursor to a dalliance if acceptable to both parties.

Number is Up

The idea of *your number being up* indicating impending death has strong links to both naval and military history but it appears the navy got there first.

1800s admirals used to summon the captains of their fleet for conference on board their flag ship by sending the *number* of their ship via semaphore signal flags. Such a summons would be seen by the entire crew and generally came shortly before action was ordered so they knew trouble beckoned.

In army parlance any soldier due for a reprimand by their commanding officer would line up outside his office, or tent, and would be called in by their *service number*. It entered into general use via the army during World War One.

Out of Your Depth

You can be literally in water which is high enough to cover your head (particularly dangerous if you can't swim to the surface) or you can figuratively be in a situation where you're barely able to cope because it's too complex, dangerous, or deep for you.

Over a Barrel

To have somebody *over a barrel* is to have the upper hand as they are rendered helpless.

There are two excellent reasons to put somebody *over a barrel* in a seafaring context. Either could be the source of this phrase which only entered printed English in 1938, but may have been around earlier.

The first option is to stretch a naughty sailor *over the barrel* before bringing out the cat o' nine tails (see the Tight Ship chapter).

The second, more likely and equally helpless option, is the common method of reviving somebody who'd nearly drowned. The unfortunate soul was placed face down *over the barrel* which was then rolled back and forth vigorously to drain the seawater from their lungs and hopefully jolt them back into breathing. It's unknown how often the *over the barrel* idea succeeded.

Barrel, despite being a very common item for centuries, has unknown origins. It was present by the 1300s in several European languages in various spellings, but the source hasn't been found although *barriclus* in Medieval Latin is a good candidate.

Push the Boat Out

To *push the boat out* in a non-nautical fashion is to spend lavishly, probably to mark a special event such as a wedding, graduation, or house warming.

Pushing boats out in the nautical fashion is literally to *push* a newly built (or recently repaired) boat out from the shore and into the water. This is usually a task requiring multiple pushers and takes the kind of generosity shown by those helping to push-start a car on a muddy road, as there's a really good chance you're going to get your trousers wet and end up hot, bothered, and mucky.

To *push the boat out* came to mean the round of drinks, or other treat, provided by the grateful boat-owner after you'd helped her or him shove the darn thing afloat.

Over time it came to mean any overly generous offer or treat, not always preceded by the kindness of strangers wading along a muddy foreshore.

Pressgang
(see also *Shanghai Press* in the Eponyms chapter)

From the 1600s the shortage of crew in a rapidly expanding Royal Navy gave the impetus to legislation making it legal to abduct members of the public to serve on board their ships. This concept was named the *pressgang* not from the idea of *pressing* or forcing the sailors, but from the French word *prest* (to lend). Under English law no contract is valid unless payment has been exchanged so a *pressed* sailor would be encouraged (either via the judicious application of free drink or the vigorous application of the cat o' nine tails) to take the king's shilling as an advance on pay and to sign the muster roll.

The drawback from a captain's perspective was a crew of landlubbers who didn't know their scuppers from their scuttle. The solution was the *High Seas Press* where short-staffed warships held up civilian merchant ships and fishing ships at cannon point and *pressed* experienced crew members.

At the time the Royal Navy didn't recognise American citizenship and the number of Americans *pressed* in this manner was a contributing factor to the War of 1812 between the two countries.

Pressgangs fell into disuse after the Napoleonic wars of 1803-1815 but it is technically still in the law books, although since 1820 you're freed from service after a mere seven years.

Sea Change

A *sea change* is always a radical shift or change, sometimes in the weather, sometimes in people or circumstances.

Sea change came from a landlubber, William Shakespeare, in his 1610 nautical play "The Tempest". Ariel sings the following lines –

> *"Full fathom five thy father lies;*
> *Of his bones are coral made;*
> *Those are pearls that were his eyes:*
> *Nothing of him that doth fade*
> *But doth suffer a sea-change*
> *Into something rich and strange."*

In that case the *sea change* was literally made by the sea, but change (regardless of cause) is more commonly understood to be the phrase's meaning now.

Sea Legs

Anybody who has ever stepped onto a raft, canoe, or ferry will know it moves around in a disconcerting fashion. Sailors find a balancing point so they can walk, and run, around decks with an ease envied by landlubbers and casual passengers. Once they've achieved this wondrous state they are said to have their *sea legs*.

When sailors steps ashore they have to repeat the process to get their *land legs*. It is unclear if this is twice as difficult for horses and other four-legged creatures transported by ship. Pity is extended to any centipede taken on a long sea voyage.

Set Your Cap At

The *cap* of a warship is its prow. When a helmsman was ordered to *set the cap* at an enemy ship it meant he had to aim his ship at them. The expression moved ashore in the 1600s and swiftly became more metaphorical. In the 1800s it became associated with women setting their matrimonial ambitions on a specific man and the idea of the *cap* became confused with a woman's hat.

Slush Fund

A *slush fund* is a useful pot of money for a rainy day but can have negative connotations too. A *slush fund* may be associated with bribes for political gain or may be seen as a store of money which is accessible without proper procedures being following and hence open to corruption.

Slush is that half-melted unpleasant state of snow and that's how it it was coined and entered English in the 1600s and now gives us flavoured ice drinks called *slushies*. The *slush* in a *slush fund* arose later and is far from pleasant to taste.

By the mid 1700s *slush* referred to the grease obtained when boiling meat on board a ship. It was described as stinking but was regarded as a major perk for the ship's cook. The cook, or other crew members, would gather *slush* by skimming it off the top of the cooking pot and storing it in spare barrels. When they reached port they'd sell the fat to tanneries and candlemakers. The money they got for it was their *slush fund*.

This idea of putting aside money, or potential money in this case, for use later became attached to *slush fund*. By 1894 politicians used *slush funds* to defeat their opponents through bribes and buying influence.

"The Simpsons" cartoon explored the nautical origins of a *slush fund* in their 1998 "Lord of the Dance" episode when Homer and Bart hatch a scheme to make money selling grease. When they try to siphon off Groundskeeper Willie's stash of rancid fat from the school's kitchen a fight breaks out as he defends his "retirement grease."

Son of a Gun

This expression was originally a way of saying someone's father was unknown, but now is an exclamation of surprise or affection.

Where there was an all male crew, there were often ladies aboard to help fulfil carnal desires. This was prevalent in the 1500-1600s in the Royal Navy and as a large portion of the crew had been pressed into service (see pressgang, above) allowing them ashore wasn't an option. Instead a group of ladies lived aboard. This practice gave us *show a leg* - the call of the bo'sun to encourage everybody still in a hammock to prove they were resting females.

Inevitably pregnancies occurred and the mother would give birth on the *gun deck*, perhaps screened by a sheet. If her baby was female both of them would be put ashore at the next port, but the Navy retained baby boys who would grow up to be cabin boys. Male births were registered in the ship's log as *a son of a gun* as the father could be any sailor.

Son of a gun was adopted in 1750s America as another way of saying son of a bitch, a phrase so popular amongst American troops in World War One that their French allies nicknamed them *Les Sommobiches*.

Swinging the Lead
{with thanks to Peter Sheehan}

In modern terms one who is *swinging the lead* is a slacker, dodging real work.

The *lead* was the leaden weight at the bottom of a line used to measure the depth of water when the ship was in shallow waters. Legend has it that managing the line was easy and a sailor *swinging the lead* was avoiding tougher tasks.

Sadly there is little evidence this particular phrase predates its first print usage in 1917 in relation to a soldier avoiding work. The phrase on board ships was actually *heaving the lead* and makes the job sound like a tough one to be avoided rather than the other way around.

The *lead* weights were up to 28 pounds in weight (or 56 pounds for deep sea fathomings) and the work would have been supervised directly by an officer so any notion of a sailor *swinging the lead* quickly and calling out an estimated depth is probably false, particularly as the sailor was on the ship which might sink if she ran aground. It was in his own personal interest to take a genuine depth sounding.

Take Soundings & Plummet
{with thanks to Peter Sheehan}

To *take soundings* is to measure the depth of water with a line attached to a lead weight, also called a *sounding lead* (explained in *swinging the lead*, above).

The expression is first noted in the late 1200s. Associating that action of checking your ship has enough water under its hull with the idea of getting to the bottom of an issue using mind power arises in English in the 1620s. A more common use in recent times is that *taking soundings* is to check for reactions to an idea before taking further action.

The same idea is in "*fathoming an idea*" as again that action was originally about checking the fathoms, or depth of water, beneath your vessel.

Taking soundings with a plumb was also used, where a *plumb* was the lead weight. It dates to the 1500s and gives us the notion of *plumbing the depths* for getting to the bottom of something (1590s).

Yet another version of the same concept was *plummet*. In the 1620s if you *plummeted* you were *taking soundings* in water using a *plummet* (1400s English) which was a ball of lead attached to a line, drawn from the Old French word *plomet* for lead or *soundings lead*.

Plummet is more common now, in aviation contexts, for a rapid fall, like a lead weight falling through water.

Tell it to the Marines

This expression - used to indicate disbelief in a tall tale - has a widely spread false origin story, and a real one which is linked to the Royal Navy.

In the fake story King Charles II (1630-1685) was told about the existence of flying fish. He insisted the story be retold to a nearby *marines* commander as they were the most widely travelled and trustworthy of his subjects. If the *marine* accepted it, then so would the king.

Unfortunately that tale isn't recorded anywhere until two hundred years later.

Much more likely is the Royal Navy usage of the correct period which was to say it in answer to a salty sea dog yarn on the basis that you might be able to fool a *marine* (soldier on a ship) but you weren't going to fool a sailor.

Tide Over

The idea of *tiding over* is to make a small allowance of money, food, or other supplies to keep someone going until stocks are replenished.

Associating such a thing with the *tides* isn't an obvious connection but it does have a salty source thanks to the original linkage of *tide* and time in the seafaring community. The quotation *tide and time waits for no man* (origin unknown but in use by 1225) springs to mind.

Tide was a synonym for *time* in the past. In a world less time-obsessed the sailor having to wait for the *tide* to float their boat and enable sailing was a way of measuring time.

Tiding over was a seafaring term used by Captain John Smith in his influential 1627 sailing manual. Captain Smith is better known for his role in establishing the first permanent English colonial settlement in North America at Jamestown, Virginia.

He explained *tiding over* as being the practice of waiting for the *tide* to float your ship in the absence of wind to fill the sails, or in the opposite case to anchor up if the *tide* wasn't with you. The idea is that a sailing ship without wind could use the force of the *tide* to get to its destination, to *tide over* to a place. They could then anchor and wait for the next useful tidal force to make more progress.

This solution to an, often temporary, obstacle to sailing, by the 1800s had given the phrase its modern meaning of *tiding over* a short term difficulty.

Toe the Line
{with thanks to Peter Sheehan}

Various occupations lay claim to the phrase *toe the line* (and no, it's not *tow the line*). British politicians have the best story, but the likeliest source is sailors.

The political legend says that to stop feisty parliamentarians in the British House of Commons two red lines were painted on the floor of the chamber, two sword lengths apart, and the opposing politicians, who were allowed to carry their swords to work, had to stay behind them when debating the points of the day. Unfortunately this is unlikely to be true. The present building was rebuilt in the 1950s after World War Two bomb damage but paintings of the earlier structure, when swords were allowed, show no such line.

In the 1800s, sailors had to line up on deck with their *toe* to a join in the boards, literally *toeing the line*, when they were to receive a group punishment and this was referenced in 1831 in print.

Toes themselves have an interesting word history. Many early languages only had one word for fingers and *toes*. In Old English the word was *ta* and the plural was *tan* which came from Mercian (language of kingdom of Mercia) and very similar to Old Norse *ta*, Old Frisian *tane*, and Middle Dutch *te*.

Touch and Go

If a situation is *touch and go* you're in a tricky spot, it could go either way, even a slight mistake could prove disastrous.

If you're an airplane pilot you might be more familiar with *touch and go* (or circuit and bumps) as the training exercise where you barely land and then immediately take off for another circuit.

The idea of *touch and go* as a precarious situation arose in the 1800s from the world of sailing ships which might give the seabed, rocks, or other obstacle a glancing blow but then continue on their course. The stakes are high. If the ship doesn't manage to proceed it could run aground or find a hole in its hull, but if the captain and crew are quick, disaster can be averted.

19. Weather

Every smart sailor keeps a close eye on the weather. The seas are large and dangerous places for a tiny boat if the wind picks up and the waves swell. As a result sailors gave us many weather words which are used both on land and at sea from *tsunami* to *hurricane*. Just be careful if you decide to whistle for a wind. You may get more than you expect.

Beaufort Scale

The *Beaufort Scale* is a measure of wind speed at sea or on land devised in 1805 by Sir Francis *Beaufort* (1774-1857) from Navan, Ireland, while he was serving on the *HMS Woolwich*, his first command as captain.

Naval officers made regular weather observations but such observations were subjective and unreliable. *Beaufort*, using earlier work by the author Daniel Defoe and others, created a wind force scale based on easily observable features such as the movement of smoke, tree foliage, and sails. Zero is dead calm. Twelve is hurricane or as Francis said "that which no canvas could withstand".

The scale was first used on the voyage of the *HMS Beagle* which is better known for Charles Darwin's work. In fact *Beaufort* had a hand in introducing Darwin to the captain of the *Beagle*. The scale was officially adopted in the 1930s.

Modern weather forecasts give windspeed as miles (or kilometres) per hour. However general public weather warnings will still use gale, storm, and hurricane – the terms from the *Beaufort Scale*.

Francis, who went to sea aged 14, was a lifelong learner and friend of Charles Babbage (inventor of the first computer) and other scientists of his day. When injured in the Napoleonic wars he spent his recuperation time setting up a semaphore link from Dublin to Galway.

He had a keen interest in accurate nautical charts having been shipwrecked at the age of 15 thanks to a bad chart. He became official hydrographer (cartographer of seas) to the Royal Navy at the age of 55, a post he held until he was 80. Some of his charts are still in use today.

His final rank in the navy was Rear Admiral and his name has been given to part of the Arctic Ocean (the *Beaufort Sea*) and *Beaufort Island* in the Antarctic.

Doldrums

To *be in the doldrums* has been used since the 1800s to indicate boredom and low spirits but in the Age of Sail it was a more serious position for a ship.

The *doldrums* are areas of light winds around 30 degrees latitude in each hemisphere in both the Pacific and Atlantic oceans. They were also called the Horse Latitudes thanks to Spanish ship's practice of throwing horses overboard when becalmed there to preserve drinking water.

The expression *flogging a dead horse* is connected both to the Horse Latitudes and to the ceremony of the Dead Horse. Sailing as far the Horse Latitudes typically took about one month which was the time it took sailors to work off their advance pay (spent ashore before the trip commenced). When the month was up they tossed a stuffed canvas horse overboard to celebrate being paid again. Captains noted that getting the crew to work hard during that month was as easy as *flogging a dead horse* into activity.

East of the Bahamas a strong current causes sargasso seaweed to cluster on the surface. This area is known as the Sargasso Sea. It rarely rains there and the winds are light to non-existent. It is often compared to a desert in the sea. Becalmed ships here often didn't survive the lack of drinking water, and the area was believed to be haunted by the ghosts of the horses and the sailors who had perished. The area is also called *the Doldrums* or the Dungeon of Lost Souls. Columbus sailed through the area with difficulty thanks to magnetic variation issues with his compass.

Hurricane

Hurricane entered the English language in the 1500s from the Spanish word *huracán*. The Spanish were busy in the Caribbean at the time thanks to the Golden Age of Sail. *Huracán* came from the Taino language where *Hurakán* was their god of evil. The Taino people were indigenous to the Caribbean and Florida. They borrowed the word from the Mayan god of wind, storm, and fire.

The god *Hurakán* sounds adorable. This one-legged creator god is sometimes depicted with a second serpent-like limb. According to legend he lived in the mists above the waters and by repeating the word "earth" he caused the land to arise. Unfortunately the humans angered him and he was equally happy to send a deluge to wash them away. The cycle of creation and eradication happened three times. He even sent a plague of turkeys and dogs at one point, perhaps that's where we get *it's raining cats and dogs*?

Spanish also gave us *tornado* (which comes from *tronado* meaning thunderstorm) and *tornar* meaning to turn.

Saint Elmo's Fire

Saint Elmo's fire is a weather phenomenon which sometimes appears on ships during thunderstorms. A glowing light, sometimes in the shape of a ball, is produced by a sharp pointed object (such as a mast or spar) in the strong electrical field. The physics behind this are similar to how neon lights glow.

Sailors regarded the lights with awe and named them for *Saint Elmo*, the patron saint of sailors. It was regarded as a good omen. Saint Nicholas is also the patron saint of sailors and Russian crews would call it *Saint Nicholas' fire*. Many have observed it through the centuries, including Charles Darwin on board *The Beagle*.

Spindrift

A hugely popular name for boats, and houses in coastal locations, *spindrift* is the evocative word for the spray of water from wave-tops during high winds.

Spindrift also describes the fine mist of sand blown along a beach, or snow blown from a hillside. The Scottish word *spoondrift* has the same meaning (coming from *spoon* meaning "to sail before the wind").

In Greek and Roman mythology Leucothea is the goddess of *spindrift*. In Homer's "Odyssey" she appears as a gannet to tell shipwrecked Odysseus to discard his cloak and raft in favour of a veil to wrap around himself in order to reach land.

Tides

Strictly speaking *tides* are not nautical weather but there's no doubt a storm combined with a high *tide* will cause more damage. The bulging of the waters towards the moon's gravity were first explained by Sir Issac Newton (1643-1727). Spring *tides* are particularly high as the gravitational pull of the moon and the sun work together during those alignments. They are not related to spring as a season.

Neap *tides* are weaker and occur when the forces of the sun and moon are perpendicular to each other. A ship can be said to be beneaped when the water doesn't flow high enough to bring it out of dock or over a sandbar.

A *rip-tide* (or *riptide*) is not a *tide*, it's a current. This compound word dates to 1862.

Tsunami

A *tsunami*, or tidal wave, is one of the most terrifying aspects of nautical weather, although technically it's a seismic occurrence rather than a weather event. A *tsunami* is a series of waves in a body of water caused by a displacement of a large volume of water. They usually happen in oceans but are possible in large lakes.

Various disturbances can trigger a *tsunami* – earthquakes, glacier calvings, underwater detonations, landslides, and meteorite impacts.

Tsunamis were named in English in 1896 to record the one which hit Japan on the 15th of June that year. It's a compound word from the Japanese words *tsu* (harbour) and *nami* (waves) which is an innocent name for something which can be so dangerous.

Calling a *tsunami* a tidal wave is somewhat misleading as unlike normal sea waves, they are not influenced by the gravitational pull of the moon. They are known as tidal waves because initially they can resemble a rapidly rising tide rather than the more usual breaking wave.

Tsunamis can travel at over 600mph (965kph) in the open sea, as fast as a jet plane, and hence can cross an ocean in a matter of hours. A wind generated wave can only travel at about 55mph (89kph) in comparison.

90% of *tsunamis* occur in the Pacific Ocean but they were known to the ancients. The Roman historian Ammimanus Marcellinus described a *tsunami* in his book after one devastated the city of Alexandria in 365 A.D. He discussed the earthquake, the sudden retreat of the sea, and then the gigantic wave. The Greek historian Thucydides suggested in his 5th century B.C. book that *tsunamis* were related to submarine earthquakes but further understanding of them remained scant until more recent times.

The most deadly *tsunami* in recent history took place in the Indian Ocean in 2004 (triggered by a 9.0 magnitude earthquake) and resulted in 230,000 people killed or missing across fourteen countries around the ocean. *Tsunamis* don't represent a threat to shipping in deep water - in 2004 only ships in port were damaged.

65 million years ago a meteor hit Mexico and formed the Chicxulub crater. The subsequent *tsunami* may have

caused the mass extinction event which wiped out the dinosaurs and other species.

Under the Weather

Under the weather is a way of saying somebody is unwell, or possibly hungover. The first victims were sailors.

Keeping watch on a ship is one of the more boring tasks and the worst station was the *weather side* where the wind blew waves onto the hapless watcher. By the end of their watch *under the weather* they'd go below soaked, cold, and vulnerable to illness. The sailor might later fall ill or die and so the association with ill-health was born. Equally a sailor feeling unwell would probably be sent *under* (below) to recover.

Whistling for a Wind

Whistling on board ship was discouraged on sailing ships. Up to 1910 whistling aboard was a punishable offence in the British navy. This was because the workings of the crew were controlled by the bosun's *whistle* and ordinary *whistling* might cause confusion.

Sailors also held a superstition that *whistling* might call the devil and bring a storm with it. However if a ship was becalmed for a prolonged period an older sailor might take his chances, sticking his knife in the mast and *whistling* for a wind.

The phrase *whistle down the wind* isn't of nautical origin. It comes from falconry and dates to the 1600s.

Wind Dog

A *wind dog* is an incomplete rainbow, usually heralding the approach of a storm at sea.

20. Salmagundi

Salmagundi is one of my favourite words. It describes a type of dish, rather than a specific recipe. The idea is that a *salmagundi* is a platter of food of many different types all arranged together, possibly with a dressing. The most basic version was boiled salt fish with onions but it could also contain chopped meat, eggs, and anything which was available to the chef. *Salmagundi* is the perfect dish for when stores are low, on a ship nearing the end of its voyage, for example.

A more luxurious version might contain turtle, fish, cabbage, grapes, spices, olives, meats etc. The dish was particularly popular amongst pirate crews but *salmagundi* spread ashore and was regularly served to peasants and kings.

In this chapter I'll serve a *salmagundi* of nautical words and phrases which defied my efforts to stow them in previous chapters. They are unique, individual, and far too good to omit from this volume. *Bon appetit!*

Ahoy!

Alexander Graham Bell (1847-1992), the Scottish scientist and co-inventor of the telephone made the very first phone call (to his co-inventor Thomas Watson). He always believed the correct way to answer the phone was with a cheerful *Ahoy!* but Thomas Edison preferred hello. By 1889 telephone exchange operators were known as hello-girls.

The hail of *ahoy* from one boat to another has murky linguistic roots. There may have been a type of boat called a *hoy*. *Hoy* was also a nautical expression used when hauling. It could have been a Viking battle cry. It may simply be a corruption of the call *Ho?* to ask to where a boat was headed.

The correct reply to *ahoy!* on the telephone, should you wish to revive the idea, is *hoy*!

Castaway

Castaway has two meanings. In nautical terms it's somebody who is shipwrecked or adrift at sea (from 1799) but on land it's somebody, or something, rejected as worthless.

The most famous *castaway* in history was Alexander Selkirk (1676-1721) who ran away to sea at the age of 19. He joined an expedition to the South Seas led by William Dampier – an explorer, navigator, and buccaneer - but when they reached the Fernández Islands, 400 miles off the coast of Chile, Selkirk fell out with his captain and asked to be put ashore. Despite changing his mind almost immediately, he was abandoned.

He lived on the uninhabited island, with a herd of wild goats for the next four years and his experiences provided huge inspiration for Daniel Defoe's iconic novel "Robinson Crusoe" (1719), which was initially rejected by several publishers.

Selkirk had been left with some basics and the rest he was able to make or grow on the island. In 1709 a British ship put in at the island and discovered a wild man, dressed in goat hides, and heard his story. They brought him home but he found it difficult to adjust to his old life and longed for the solitude of the island. He married twice but eventually returned to life at sea and died in the service of the Royal Navy.

Selkirk, the real Crusoe, never had a Man Friday on his island.

Cenotaph

Cenotaphs were first created in ancient Greece. They were monuments to those lost at sea and were always erected on headlands. The word is compounded from two Greek words – *kenos* (empty) and *taphos* (tomb) which makes tragic sense as the sea doesn't always yield up the bodies of those she takes.

The most famous *cenotaph* in the U.K. stands in Whitehall, London since 1920 and was designed by Sir Edward Lutyens to commemorate those who died in World War One.

Ditty Bag

Admittedly this term is not in common use on land, but it should be as it's a much better name than sewing kit.

By the 1800s, every sailor had a small bag containing needles, thread, thimble, and scissors for mending and altering their clothes. The clothes provided by the purser were invariably ill-fitting and sailors soon learned how to adjust them. Their little bag of sewing sundries was named the *ditty bag*, possibly after a British naval phrase *commodity bag*.

Gillie

A *gillie* (or *ghillie*) is a guide on angling or deer stalking trips, especially in Scotland or Ireland. They use local knowledge to advise on tactics, equipment, and locations to visiting fishermen and hunters.

The word dates to the 1500s and comes from Scots Gaelic *gille* (lad or servant) and Irish *giolla*. The terms were used for a chief's attendant further back in the past.

One obsolete variant is the *ghillie-weetfit* (*gillie caisfliuch* in Gaelic, literally wet foot) whose duty was to carry his master over streams and boggy patches, a very useful service in the typically damp conditions of the Scottish and Irish highlands. The term became one of contempt as being the one doing the carrying wasn't exactly high-status employment.

Gizmo

Gizmo as a word for anything you can't put a name to (like thingamajig and thingamabob etc.) entered English in 1942 thanks to the Marine and Naval services. Its origins are unknown but it's likely to be an invented word.

Gongoozle
{With thanks to Clíodna Johnston}

A *gongoozler* (gon-goos-ler) is one who watches people messing about in boats, canal boats to be specific. This rare word only entered English in the early 1900s, possibly from the Lincolnshire dialect word *gooze*, to stare or gape.

Heave-Ho!

Heave-Ho! is a common call in sea shanties but to understand what it means you have to explore the two parts individually.

Heave entered Old English as *hebban* from German, Dutch, and Old Norse roots all with the same meaning of lift or take up, but with a variety of different spellings. It was only in 1944 that *heave* took on the second meaning of a dismissal.

Ho is always an interjection of some sort. English has numerous version from *gung-ho* (see the Flying the Flag chapter) to *heigh-ho* and *tally-ho*. Using a series of *ho-ho-ho* to indicate laughter dates back to the 1100s, probably thanks to Saint Nicholas.

Ho used with a place name (for example, *Westward-Ho*) was used by boatmen to indicate departure for that place from the 1500s and *ho* would have been used solo from the 1300s to attract attention and demand silence, for example to stop chatter amongst the crew.

These two nautical versions of *ho* give us the clue for *heave-ho* – the call to work demanded the hands listen for the rhythmic call of when to lift or pull (for example a large sail, a new mast, a net full of fish, or the anchor). Each time the caller said *Heave*, they'd pull, then the *Ho* was the pause. The call was repeated, perhaps with the addition of a sea shanty for morale and team rhythm, until the task was completed.

In more recent land-based usage to get the *heave-ho* is to be dismissed from your work or relationship.

Junk

A *junk* is a flat bottomed sailing boat from the Far East. She has no keel, a high stern, and her rudder can be raised or lowered. The two or three masts carry battened square sails which used to be made from bamboo, rattan, or woven grass. Easy to steer and good at sea, the *junk* was the vessel of choice for Far Eastern pirates for centuries.

The word *junk* for this type of ship entered English in the late 1500s from the Portuguese word *junco*, but originally from the Malay word *jong* or *djong* (large boat).

The word *junk* which is now used to describe rubbish also comes from the sea, but not from the eastern sailing ship. *Junk* entered English spelled as *junke* in the 1300s to describe the oddments of rope which were used to caulk gaps in the boat's planking. That type of *junk* came from Old French *junc* (rush or reed) for something of little value and originally from Latin *iuncus* (reed).

By the 1660s junk described refuse from boats and by 1884 it referred to rubbish of any kind, but usually with an implication of being re-used later. The original *junk shop* was actually called a marine shop in 1800, a place for selling items discarded from a ship. This later gave us *junk art* (1961), *junk food* (1971), and a surprisingly early dictionary entry for *junk mail* (1954).

Marine, Mariner, Marina, and Marinade

Marine is the earliest of these words to venture into English. It was used as a noun for sea coast from the 1300s from the Old French *marin* (of the sea, maritime) and ultimately from Latin *marinus* (of the sea) and *mare* (sea).

By the 1660s, *marine* could be used to describe shipping as a whole. The idea of a *marine* being a soldier serving on a ship came directly from French *marine* (see also *tell it to the marines* in the Phrases chapter). There's also *mariner* for sailor and *submarine* was compounded in the 1640s.

A *marina* comes from the same roots but originally described a promenade by the sea (1805). It didn't describe a docking area for yachts and small boats until American English adopted it in 1935.

The same roots also give us *marinade* (1704), as foods were originally pickled in salted water, brine, or vinegar and salt water was associated with the sea.

Mark Twain

Mark Twain is the call a Mississippi riverboat hand will make when taking depth soundings and has been in U.S. nautical use since 1799. A *mark* was the same as a fathom at sea (about six feet) and *twain* means two. *Twain* came from the Old English word *twegen* from Proto-Germanic.

Mark Twain meant the riverboat had a depth of twelve feet beneath her, a clear channel.

Samuel Langhorne Clemens (1835-1910) was a Mississippi riverboat pilot for four years before he took *Mark Twain* as his pen name and created classics like "The Adventures of Huckleberry Finn" and 27 other books plus journalism and short fiction collections.

Mollgogger

A *mollgogger* was a roller, or pair of rollers, at the gunwale of a mine sweeper ship. Such vessels towed a large number of lines from the stern and needed to keep them straight and untangled, which was the *mollgogger's* job. A rare word now, it has been adopted as the name of sea shanty singing group from Cork, Ireland.

Monitor

The original *monitor* in English (1540s onwards) is a school pupil who is put in charge of their peers and younger students to enforce rules. *Monitor* in English is a direct acquisition from the Latin word with the same meaning.

However, after its school days, *monitor* gained watery roots before becoming the term for a computer screen or TV screen (1930s).

In 1826 the *monitor* lizard was so named because it was rumoured to give warning to humans about the approach of Nile crocodiles. Then in 1862 John Ericsson (1803-1889) invented an iron-clad slow moving warship and named the first one launched *The Monitor* because he wanted it to admonish the confederate side in the American Civil War.

By the time television was invented the idea of a screen showing the feed from a single camera, for quality and editing purposes, was naturally called a *monitor* and a screen attached to a computing system also needed a window to check it was operating correctly, hence the *monitor* there.

Posh
{with thanks to Paddy "PJ" Callahan}

While there is no hard evidence for the origins of *posh* as a word to indicate somebody or something is upperclass or glamourous, a widely accepted nautical story exists.

The word *posh* began to be used in 1914 and may have roots in thieves slang of the late 1800s. Alternatively, wealthy British passengers travelling on the P&O Lines to India were assigned cabins on the *port* side of the ship on the outward voyage and on the *starboard* side on the return journey in order to avoid the worst of the sun's heat during the day. As a result their tickets were stamped *POSH – Port Out Starboard Home.* In an era before air-conditioning you can see why they might pay a premium for those tickets.

Proof
{with thanks to @IrishSmuggling on Twitter}

On bottles of alcohol you will often see its *proof* level listed. This term comes to the drinks trade thanks to suspicious sailors, smugglers, and importers in the 1500s, with a little help from the taxman.

At that time, spirits were taxed at different rates depending on their strength. Before the invention of the specific gravity test in 1816, the best way to determine, or *prove*, the alcohol content of your cask was to soak a pellet of gunpowder in the liquid. If the gunpowder could still ignite the spirits were rated as *above proof* and taxed on the higher rate. Such drinks were listed as *100 degrees proof* and had an alcohol content of 57%, or higher, by modern standards.

Quarantine

Quarantine has two distinct usages. The earliest doesn't have nautical links. The *quarantine* (1520s) was the period of forty days a widow was allowed to stay in her husband's home after his death. The custom was named after the *quarantyne* – when Christ fasted for forty days in the desert in the Bible. It was originally named from *quattour* (four) in Latin. The widow's *quarantine* allowed her a space to grieve and arrange her finances before pressure could be applied for her to pay rent and it dates to the Magna Carter (1215). This was quoted in legal proceedings as recently as 1986 in the Michigan Court of Appeals.

The version of *quarantine* with watery roots is the medical kind and is claimed by Venice, although other cities lent a hand. The first medical *quarantine* in written history is against leprosy when in the book of Leviticus it is stated that they are unclean and must stay outside the camp. The word *quarantine* wasn't used yet. It took the Black Death to give us that.

In the 1300s waves of plague swept across Europe, killing up to a third of the population. Desperate measures were taken to contain the spread of the disease. For example, the Viscount of Reggio ordered that all sufferers be taken out of the city to the fields and left to die or recover.

The Great Council of Ragusa (now Dubrovnik, Croatia) established a place outside the city walls to treat the ill and contain incomers who might be infected. Their law, with detailed month-long isolation rules, was called the *trentino*.

During the next 80 years similar laws were introduced in other port cities – Genoa, Marseilles, and Venice. The period was extended from 30 to 40 days, perhaps as a reference to Christ's 40 days in the desert and the period of Lent. As a result the laws were called *quarantino* (quarantine).

In Venice the *quarantine* (1377) required ships arriving from infected ports to anchor for 40 days before landing goods or crew. This usage was extended to mean any period of extended isolation for medical reasons in the 1670s.

Rosemary

The herb *rosemary's* name derives from Latin, *rosmarinus*. *Rosmarinus* is compounded from *ros* (dew) and *marinus* (sea). *Rosemary* was called dew of the sea because it grew near the sea.

Rosemary, as well as its culinary uses, is associated with improved memory (Greek scholars entwined it in their hair when studying) and has the association of being "for remembrance" (as mentioned by Ophelia in "Hamlet" by William Shakespeare) so may be included in wreaths for graves.

Rosemary was also used in bridal bouquets. Anne of Cleves (1515-1557), Henry VIII's fourth wife, wore *rosemary* at their wedding. This was to symbolise love and faithfulness but also to mark remembrance of the woman's former life before marriage.

Strike

The original meaning of *strike* is to make level and smooth. The word arrived in Old English as *striccan* with influences from various German, Dutch, and Norse words with similar senses and spellings.

In a nautical context to *strike the sails* is to lower them and smooth them away until needed later. It's that nautical action which gives English the noun *strike* for an industrial dispute when workers down tools until their demands are met by their employer.

In 1768 London a docker's dispute in the East End gave English the word *strike,* and cost seven men their lives. The industrial revolution was in full swing, with workers moving from the fields to the cities, and the East End of London was crammed with workers. King George III persisted in installing his personal favourites as Prime Minister causing political riots.

Coal fuelled industry and came by canal barges to the East End where heavers, mostly Irish immigrants, worked long hours loading it onto ships. Their employers, called undertakers, also owned the bars where they drank. The undertakers charged well for the booze. Workers, who even had to rent their shovels from the bosses, sometimes ended up owing money at the end of the week to the undertakers. When new equipment reduced the number of men needed, anger flared amongst the workers.

The heavers boarded the coal ships, climbing the rigging, and *struck the sails*. They also removed the top masts confining most of the fleet of London to port, a disaster for the shipowners. Fights broke out between the sailors and heavers and several were killed. The army was sent in and seven of the heavers were hung as a lesson to the others.

1841 gave us the first use of *strike* in a baseball context. In 1942 *strike* took on another meaning – a sudden military attack.

Conclusion

In recent times with air travel and the internet it is easy to forget the importance of the sea both now and in the past. The oceans are the bridges between countries and continents. The majority of goods are still moved worldwide on ships.

Researching this book convinced me that sailors have wielded greater influence on the English language than any cluster of playwrights (with the exception of Shakespeare), journalists, or authors. The crews of ships, especially during the Age of Sail, were drawn from many nations and had to deal with a vast diversity of cultures at the ports they visited. Words and phrases were adopted by the sea dogs and brought home for inclusion in the English dictionary.

While I loved exploring the origins of nautical sayings and the vibrancy of pirate slang, my favourite experience during the writing of this book was finding words and phrases with marine roots in surprising shore use. I never thought I'd be including hazing, jingoism, cyber, and slush fund in the same book as avast, shanty, cutlass, and schooner.

I hope you enjoyed our linguistic journey on the high seas. If, like me, you're a landlubber you should now have the words to pass as a seasoned sailor and furl your skyscraper with the best of them.

Thanks

Since 2009 I've played with unusual words every week on the Wordfoolery blog (https://wordfoolery.wordpress.com). A wonderful community of readers enrich the blog with word suggestions and their passion for language. Without them this book wouldn't exist.

A number of friends and fellow wordfools suggested words for inclusion in this book, you will see their names beside the words they suggested. Many thanks to Peter Sheehan, Brendan Tierney, Nell Jenda, Rick Ellrod, Kimberly Sullivan, ZZNewell, Christine Byrne Carroll, Paul Powell, Rita Fitzsimons, Paddy "PJ" Callahan, IrishSmuggling, and Clíodna Johnston.

Thanks also to Noelle and Paddy for endless cake and encouragement at our writing group.

Every November I take part in NaNoWriMo (National Novel Writing Month), as a writer and mentor to the Ireland NorthEast region which is filled with amazing writers of all ages and genres. NaNoWriMo 2016 enabled me to draft "How To Get Your Name In The Dictionary" and NaNoWriMo 2018 saw me draft this book. If you've ever thought of writing a book, I urge you to try NaNoWriMo at www.nanowrimo.org. You get a whole thirty days to write 50,000 words.

This book is dedicated to my Dad who made the mistake of leaving large history books around our house when I was a child. They lit a spark that has yet to blow out.

Love and thanks always to Brendan, Daniel, and Eleanor.

References

Here's a selection of the resources I used to find and explore the nautical phrases and words. As a non-sailor I relied heavily on research to understand the differences between various vessels and rigging systems. Any mistakes are mine.

Special mention goes to Etymology Online (www.etymonline.com) which is a marvellous place for anybody with an interest in the English language. If you enjoy nautical myths and legends, I suggest you read more in the excellent book, "The Fabled Coast".

- "Boatowner's Sheet Anchor" by Carl D. Lane, 1969, Hawthorn Books (USA)
- "Following the Shoals" by Pat Nolan, 2010, The History Press (Ireland)
- 'The Lifeboat Service in Ireland" by Nicholas Leech, 2012, Amberley Publishing (UK)
- "The Glenans Manual of Sailing" by Peter Davison, 1995, David & Charles (UK)
- "Explore Islands of Ireland", unknown author(s), 2016, Fáilte Ireland (Ireland)
- "Breverton's Nautical Curiosities" by Terry Breverton, 2010, Quercus (UK)
- "Sticklers, Sideburns & Bikinis" by Graeme Donald, 2008, Osprey Publishing (UK)
- "Seascapes" by Tom McSweeney, 2008, Mercier Press (Ireland)
- "The Fabled Coast" by Sophia Kingshill and Jennifer Westwood, 2012, Arrow Books (UK)
- www.merriam-webster.com
- www.collinsdictionary.com

- www.dictionary.cambridge.org
- www.dictionary.com
- www.wikipedia.org
- www.phrases.org.uk
- www.mariner.ie
- https://blog.oup.com (Oxford University Press blog)
- www.space.com
- www.britannica.com
- www.christinedemerchant.com (boat building enthusiast)
- www.pirateglossary.com
- www.nationalgeographic.org
- www.rmg.co.uk (Royal Museum, Greenwich, U.K.)
- www.dockwalk.com
- www.grammar-monster.com
- https://oceanservice.noaa.gov (U.S. National Ocean Service)
- www.thewayofthepirates.com
- https://www.rte.ie/radio1/seascapes/ (RTE's maritime radio show)
- www.encyclopedia.com
- www.sciencedaily.com
- www.ancient.eu (Ancient History Encyclopaedia)
- www.thepirateking.com
- www.phrases.com
- www.marktwainmuseum.org
- www.surfing-waves.com/surf_talk.htm

About the Author

Grace Tierney (www.gracetierney.com) is a columnist, author, and blogger writing on Ireland's coast. She is the Ireland North East organiser for National Novel Writing Month (www.NaNoWriMo.org) and actually enjoys the challenge of writing 50,000 words in one month. She blogs about unusual words at http://wordfoolery.wordpress.com, tweets @Wordfoolery, and serialises contemporary comic fiction at www.channillo.com. Her first book about words "How To Get Your Name In The Dictionary" (2018) explores the extraordinary lives of those who gave their names as eponyms to English – from cardigan to casanova.

Her favourite word from the sea is gollywobbler because it sounds so silly.

https://twitter.com/Wordfoolery - writing & unusual words
www.facebook.com/gracetierneywriter - writing / life
www.instagram.com/wordfoolery/ – history through photos
www.pinterest.co.uk/GraceTierneyIrl/ - crafts, writing, history

If You Enjoyed This Book

Grace blogs every week about the history of unusual words on Wordfoolery (http://wordfoolery.wordpress.com). Drop by, all word-lovers are welcome. She takes requests so if you have a favourite obscure word, suggest it. Upcoming books inspired by the blog include "Words the Vikings Gave Us", "Words the Greeks Gave Us", "Words the French Gave Us", etc.

The easiest way to thank an author of any book, but especially one who wears the indie-publisher hat, is to post an honest review. It makes a huge difference to the visibility of the book and future sales, so if you enjoyed this romp through nautical nouns and floating phrases, please take a couple of minutes to review it. Thank you so much.

If you like ship names from ark to schooner and the stories behind them – you'll find a free download called Various Vessels on the Wordfoolery blog. Handy if you don't know your *dhows* from your *ketches*. https://wordfoolery.files.wordpress.com/2020/05/various-vessels-pdf.pdf

Index

Above board	206
Admiral	66
Aft	6
Ahoy	246
All at sea	161
All hands on deck	207
America	162
Anchor	6
Anchors aweigh	207
Aphrodisiac	105
Aran sweaters	106
Astrolabe	163
Atlantis	45
Avast	148
Baggywinkle	7
Bail	98
Bait	79
Ballast	7
Bandana	149
Barnacle	54
Batten down, see Hatch	27
Beaufort scale	238
Belay	8
Bell-bottomed trousers	202
Below & beneath	10
Bends & Decompress	55
Bermuda shorts	107
Berth	9
Between the devil and the deep blue sea	208
Bikini	108
Bilge	11
Binnacle	11
Bitter end & end of one's rope	208
Blazer	109

Blue flag	190
Blue peter	191
Bollard	122
Booby prize / booby trap	209
Boom	12
Bootcamp	184
Booty	150
Bosun & his whistle & chair	66
Bow	12
Bowsprit	13
Breeches buoy	202
Bridge	13
Brig	14
Bristol fashion	110
Brought up short	209
Buccaneer	150
Bulkhead	14
Bumpkin	14
Bunk	15
Bunting	191
Buoy	123
Burn your boats	210
By and large	210
Cabin	15
Cable	16
Caboose	16
Calenture	47
Capstan	16
Captain	68
Careen	99
Cargo	17
Castaway	247
Castoffs	203
Cat o'nine tails	184
Caul	47
Causeway	123
Cenotaph	248

Chart	163
Chock-a-block	211
Clean bill of health	212
Clearing the decks	176
Close quarters	176
Cloud cleaver	135
Coasteering	86
Cockpit	18
Cold - freeze the balls off brass monkey	212
Commodore	68
Coral	55
Cormorant	89
Corsair	151
Cowabunga	86
Coxswain	68
Crack on	135
Crew & crewcut	69
Crow's nest	18
Cruise	99
Current & currency	56
Cut and run	177, 213
Cutlass	152
Cut to the chase	214
Cyber	164
Davy Jones' locker	110
Dead in the water	214
Dead man's chest	214
Deadwood	215
Deck	19
Decompress – see the Bends	55
Derrick	112
Devil to pay and no pitch hot	215
Ditty bag	248
Dock	124
Doldrums	239
Doubloon	153
Dressing down	216

Drown	57
Ebb	57
Eddy	58
Enough to make a sailor a pair of pants	216
Estuary & Fjord	124
Faffing	217
Fairway	165
False colours, sail under	198
Fastitocalon & jasconye	90
Fathom out something	165
Fender	22
Figurehead	22
Filibuster	153
First rate	217
Fish stinks from the head down	218
Fjord – see estuary & fjord	124
Flaking out	219
Flap, in a	192
Float	100
Flogging a dead horse	240
Flotsam & jetsam	125
Fluke, whale or anchor	80
Flying colours	192
Flying jib	136
F'o'c'sle, forecastle	23
Foghorn	24
Footloose	136
Fudge the books	113
Furl	137
Gabion	126
Gaff & gaffe	24
Gale – see Beaufort Scale	238
Galley	21
Galoot	70
Gangplank/gangway	21
Get a word in edgeways	219
Gibraltar	113

Gillie	249
Gimlette	114
Give no quarter	154
Gizmo	249
Gnarly	87
Go belly up	81
Go by the board	220
Gollywobbler	137
Gongoozle	249
Governor	70
Grapnel, anchor	25
Gravlax	80
Grog & groggy	114
Groin	126
Grommets & idlers	71
Groundswell	58
Gulf	127
Gung Ho	220
Gunner	72
Gunwale	25
Halcyon Days	48
Halyard	26
Hammock	26
Hand over fist	221
Harbour	127
Hard and fast	221
Hatch & batten down the hatches	27
Haven	128
Hazing	185
Head	28
Heave-ho	250
Helmsman / helm	72
High and dry	221
High profile	222
High seas	222
Hitched & Tying the Knot	193
Hook, line, and sinker	82

Hook or by crook	115
Hot pursuit	178
Hull	29
Hunky dory	117
Hurricane	240
In the offing	223
IPA	117
Jetsam – see flotsam & jetsam	125
Jetty	128
Jib	138
Jib of Jibs	138
Jigger sail	139
Jingoism	178
Joe, cup of	118
Jolly roger	194
Jump ship	223
Junk	251
Keel	29
Keelhaul	185
Kelpie	91
Kettle of fish	224
Kissing the gunner's daughter	186
Kites	139
Knell	48
Knock off	225
Knot	195
Know the ropes	196
Kraken	92
Lagoon	129
Landlubber or lubber	65
Lanyard	203
Larboard - see Port & Portugal	130
Launch	100
Leeway	101
Leviathan	49
Lifeline	30
Line	30

Lodestar	166
Log	30
Longitude & latitude	166
Longshoreman & Stevedore	73
Loose cannon	225
Loose end	226
Luff, aluf, aloof	140
Lug sail	139
Maelstrom – see whirlpool	63
Making a pass	226
Mainstay	31
Marine, mariner, marina, and marinade	251
Mark Twain	252
Maroon	186
Mast	31
Master - see captain	68
Mate	73
Mayday	167
Mermaid	92
Mizenmast	32
Mollgogger	253
Monitor	253
Moonraker	141
Mooring	129
Mutiny	187
Nail colours to the mast	197
Nausea	93
Neptune	119
Nipper	74
Number is up	227
Octopus	94
Odyssey	50
Orlop	32
Out of your depth	227
Over a barrel	228
Overhaul	102
Paddle	32

Painter	33
Panic stations	179
Pegleg	155
Periscope	59
Petty officer	75
Pieces of eight	156
Pier	129
Pig	95
Pilot	75
Pipe down – see bo'sun	66
Piping hot – see bo'sun	66
Pirate	156
Plain sailing	168
Plimsoll	119
Plummet - see take soundings	234
Pontoon	130
Poop deck	33
Port & Portugal	130
Porthole	34
Poseidon	51
Posh	254
Pressgang, see also Shanghai press (120)	229
Privateer	157
Proof	254
Propeller	34
Prow	35
Purser	76
Push the boat out	228
Put a pin in it – see belay	8
Quadrant	169
Quarantine	255
Quartermaster	76
Quay	132
RADAR	170
Ratlines	35
Rats	95
Red flag / bloody flag	197
Red herring	82

Reef & Reefer 141
Regatta 180
Rigout 204
Ripple 59
Riptide – see tides 242
Room to swing a cat – see cat o' nine tails 184
Rosemary 256
Rostrum 181
Royal sail 142
Rudder 36
Sail under false colours 198
Saint Elmo's fire 241
Salmagundi 157
Salt 52
Salvage 102
Scuba 60
Scupper 36
Scurvy 158
Scuttle & Scuttlebutt 37
Sea change 230
Sea dogs 52
Sea legs 230
Selkie 96
Set your cap at 231
Sextant 171
Shanghaied / Shanghai press 120
Shanty 103
Shark 84
Ship-shape – see Bristol fashion 110
Shiver me timbers 159
Shot across the bows 181
Sink 60
Siren 53
Skipper 78
Sky sail 142
Skyscraper 143
Sloppy 204

Slush fund	231
Snorkel	61
SONAR	172
Son of a gun	232
SOS	172
Spanker	143
Spar & sparring	37
Spindrift	241
Spinnaker	144
Splice	198
Starboard	38
Steerage	173
Steering wheel	38
Stern	39
Stevedore – see longshoreman	73
Strike	256
Submarine	61
Sunstones	174
Swab	39
Sweet fanny adams	121
Swinging the lead	233
Tack	174
Tackle	39
Taken aback	144
Take down a peg or two	199
Take soundings	234
Tarpaulin	40
Tattoo	205
Tell it to the marines	235
Three sheets to the wind	144
Tide	242
Tide over	235
Tight ship	183
Tiller	41
Time ball	175
Toe the line	236
Tombstoning	87

Ton, Tonne, Tun	41
Topgallant	145
Topside	42
Torpedo	61
Touch and go	237
Trident	181
Tube & Tubular	88
Turn a blind eye	182
Tsunami	242
Under the weather	244
Union Jack	199
Vexillology	200
Walk the plank	159
Wardroom	42
Waster	78
Watch	188
Wave	62
Whale	96
Wharf	132
Whelmed	104
Whirlpool & Maelstrom	63
Whistling for a wind	244
Wind dog	245
Windlass	43
Yard & Yardarm	146
Yellow flag	201

Grace Tierney's Other Books

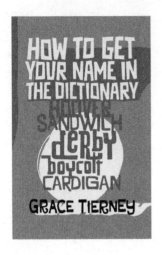

"How To Get Your Name In The Dictionary" (2018) is a light-hearted look at the lives of the soldiers, inventors, style icons, and villains who gave their names to the English language as eponyms. From atlas to zeppelin English is full of words named for Greek gods, explorers, serious scientists, and crafty chefs. These heroes and heroines, scattered through world history, all did something extraordinary to squeeze their name into the dictionary, and this book celebrates their biographies.

More than **260 eponyms** are featured across subjects as diverse as food, Irish history, calendars, hats, inventions, words named after places, Greek gods, military history, politics, astronomy, fashion, popular phrases, villains, science, and a selection of eponyms which simply defy categorisation. Widely available in paperback and ebook.

Coming Soon in the Words Series!

"Words The Vikings Gave Us"

"Words The French Gave Us"

"Words War Gave Us"

"Words The Greeks Gave Us"

"Words The Romans Gave Us"

"Words Publishing Gave Us"

"Words Asia Gave Us"

"Words The Germans Gave Us"

"Hamster Stew & Other Stories" is a diary-style comedy serial about the adventures of an Irish mom, Trish McTaggart, struggling with her teenage son, a scary ten year old daughter, and an out of control life which lurches from disaster to chaos.

All she wants is a part-time job, more passion with her Scottish husband, and a hands-off mother-in-law but life, and her daughter, are conspiring against her dreams. Perhaps the lessons her friend is giving her in "how to say no" will help?

Available to read on www.Channillo.com, the subscription reading platform (think Netflix for books). First chapter is free to read.

"Nit Roast & Other Stories" is a first person, diary-style comedy serial about the adventures of an Irish mom. This is a sequel to "Hamster Stew & Other Stories".

Trish McTaggart's family life is still a mess. Her diary holds her worries – an animal-obsessed daughter, a teen son drinking, an absent-minded husband, and a local parent who's out to get her. Building her new sewing business will be the easy part this year.

Available to read on www.Channillo.com, the subscription reading platform (think Netflix for books). First chapter is free to read.

"The Librarian's Secret Diary"

Nina is the new librarian on the block. She's learning the shelves with her buzzword-spouting boss and the senior librarian who hates reading and can't wait to retire.

She records the crazy reader requests and the knitting group in-fighting in her secret diary while trying to get the printer to work, flirting with the inter-library-loan guy, and struggling to discover why their romance books are acquiring red pen marks on page five.

Available to read on www.Channillo.com, the subscription reading platform (think Netflix for books). First chapter is free to read.

Printed in Great Britain
by Amazon